Celebration
GRAPHICS
SOURCEBOOK

Festive designs from all cultures

ROCKPORT

First published in the
United States of America by
Rockport Publishers, a member of
Quayside Publishing Group
100 Cummings Center
Suite 406-L
Beverly, Massachusetts 01915-6101
Telephone: (978) 282-9590
Fax: (978) 283-2742
www.rockpub.com

ISBN-13: 978-1-59253-589-7
ISBN-10: 1-59253-589-5

10 9 8 7 6 5 4 3 2 1

Art Direction: Tony Seddon
Design: Emily Portnoi
Typeset in Clarendon BT
and Poynter Gothic

Printed in China by 1010 Printing
International Ltd.

Celebration
GRAPHICS
SOURCEBOOK

Festive designs from all cultures

BEVERLY MASSACHUSETTS

ROCKPORT PUBLISHERS

John Stones

Contents

★ ★

Introduction

★ ★

If you look up the word "celebrate" in the *New Oxford American Dictionary*, what you will read is "mark (a significant or happy day or event), typically with a social gathering." The word "mark" is important: very often such events involve a literal marking—a graphic act of some sort or another. Some of the oldest images of humanity, the cave paintings of prehistoric man, most probably had a ceremonial function. It is something that has continued right through to the modern day, and the significant moments in our lives assume much of their meaning and richness from the visuals that accompany them, whether they be in the shape of a greeting card, a banner, or a public display.

While graphics sometimes play a supporting role—to create a relevant and decorative backdrop—on other occasions they assume a central role and almost become the event itself. Take Valentine's Day, where the card more or less *is* the celebration. And while cards, or other printed items, make up the majority of what we call celebration graphics, there are also many other manifestations, from the painting of people's own bodies to decorating the sky with patterns created by fireworks or fighter jets, from gift wrap to street banners to animated store displays.

Today, graphic design is often used for marketing communications, and even though many of the projects in this book have a clear commercial purpose—whether to promote a business or product, or be salable themselves—they are not reducible to commercial imperatives. When it comes to celebrations and festivities, graphic design participates in an older tradition of visually expressing and creating communal meaning. While some of these graphic designs may seem trifles, they are also images that punctuate time, give our lives a sense of meaning and community, and lend our cultures identity.

While the visual is part and parcel of most celebrations, some cultures and religions place more emphasis on it than others. For instance, modern Christianity is generally more than happy to express its festivities and events through visual representations, but Judaism has a strict iconoclasm at its heart following the command set out in Exodus 20:4: "Thou shalt not make unto thee any graven image, or any likeness of any thing that is in heaven above, or that is in the earth beneath, or that is in the water under the earth." This means that Jewish culture prioritizes the textual over the visual, and its major events do not have the same visual expression as many others.

Likewise, Islam has a widely adhered to tenet against the representation of living beings, but instead relies on a rich, largely abstract and generic visual vocabulary.

Contemporary society in general, however, is far from iconoclastic: it consumes images at an alarming rate, whether by encountering advertising; browsing online; watching television; going shopping; or reading books, newspapers, and magazines. While it surrounds us, as a society generally we find it hard to value this visual discourse and those who create it.

Children may be taught how to spell a word, but there won't necessarily be the same attention given to describing its iconography. The iconography, or visual toolkit that makes up an event, is taken for granted. But for the designer wishing to create a festive graphic, this needs to be understood and investigated, even if some of it may be assumed to have been absorbed symbiotically.

★ ★

In our digital times, the death of print is often announced, but celebration graphics are a definite thorn in the side of this belief. People are still very much attached to the idea of a tangible card, some 7 billion a year of which are sent every year in the USA, according to the Greeting Card Association. And despite so much of our lives migrating online, and the proliferation of sites offering e-cards, they make up only a tiny proportion of the cards we send. According to Hallmark, the giant US greeting card company, printed cards outnumber e-cards by a factor of 20 to 1. While the dangers of spam and viruses might be a contributing factor, the real reason is that for many an e-mail simply doesn't feel as special or as festive as a printed card. Nevertheless, what we are exposed to on our screens is part of our environment, and we have included some examples of the digital expressions of celebration, whether festive wallpapers or e-cards, that will become more prevalent.

While the medium may be old, the festivities can be surprisingly young. Events can very quickly become part of the landscape. Take the Afro-American festivity of Kwanzaa established in the 1960s,

or World AIDS Day, first held in the 1980s, and likewise the music festivals that grew out of the counter-cultural movements of the 1960s, whose enduring appeal is perhaps due to their continuity with older festive traditions. These new celebrations show how culture is in constant flux rather than something to be viewed like an ethnographic exhibit in a museum. It is our little actions, often visual, that keep this stream flowing.

Professional graphic design has an important role to play in this, even as it coexists or overlaps with folkloric and craft traditions. When it comes to celebration graphics, there is a certain democracy at play: famous graphic designers compete for our attention and emotions on a level playing field with the crayon-drawn creations of children at kindergarten and the uncredited designers of cards for the major card manufacturers.

This book is a compendium of tools and images for the celebration and expression of important events in our times. Many of the events will have a basic established and evolving visual vocabulary or iconography, which we present along with a description of the event. It is necessarily partial and incomplete—it would be impossible

to include all the important events— but we have endeavored to present some of the most important from a visual perspective.

The projects are presented month by month, with two additional sections to cover events that can happen at any time of year, notably weddings, and birthdays and anniversaries. A quick note about calendars: while the Gregorian calendar is the internationally accepted reference point, other older traditions remain beyond its homogenizing stamp. The Gregorian calendar is arithmetical, putting it at variance with the older lunar and solar calendars from which many ancient and important celebrations, such as Ramadan and Easter, still take their reference. As a consequence their date will vary from year to year, and even geographically, and will always need to be checked with an authoritative source.

January

Sydney Festival – arts festival, Sydney, Australia

Fasching – arts festival, Munich, Germany

Carnaval de Blancos y Negros – street festival, San Juan de Pasto, Columbia

1st: New Year (pp 010–019)

10th: Voodoo Festival – Benin

Summer City Festival – arts festival, Wellington, New Zealand

16th: Festa di Sant'Antonio Abate – saint's day/bonfire night, Nuoro Province, Sardinia, Italy

25th: Burns Night – celebration of the life and poetry of Robbie Burns, Scotland

Kiruna Snow Festival – winter festival, Sweden

26th: Australia Day – Australia's independence day

Last Tuesday: Up-Helly-Aa – Viking fire festival, Shetland Islands, Scotland

Chinese New Year (pp 020–023)

New Year Gift

★ ★ ★ ★ ★ ★ ★ ★ ★ ★ ★ ★ ★ ★ ★

Design
Kanella Arapoglou

Client
Self-initiated

Format
Chocolate box calendar

Country
Greece

To wish her clients a "Happy and Sweet 2009," Greek designer Kanella Arapoglou decided to send them a box of chocolates with a difference—it would also function as a calendar of sorts. The box, held closed with a monogrammed, black wax seal, contained 12 bars of chocolate, one for each month of the year. Each was decorated with an image relevant to the month, with February featuring roses in reference to Valentine's Day. The design is executed in black dots, following the corporate identity of Kanella's studio in Athens. The back of each individual pack contains information about the illustration. The idea is that each bar is consumed by the end of the month it refers to.

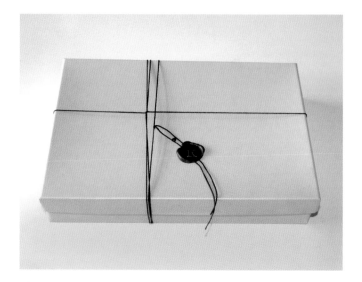

FESTIVAL FACTS

TRADITIONAL CENTRAL EUROPEAN NEW YEAR'S EMBLEMS

In European countries, especially Austria, a complex assemblage of good-luck emblems has evolved to furnish the celebration of the first day of the New Year and the final day of the old, or *Silvester* as it is called in German. Used in two- or three-dimensional depictions, the following emblems feature on cards, table displays, confectionary wrappers, invitations, and so on.

- **Four-leaf clover:** a rare mutation, finding one is seen as good luck in many cultures.

- **Chimney sweep:** there are various legends to explain why the young chimney sweep should be lucky, but most credible is the fact that after his visit the air inside the home would be fresher.

- **Toadstool mushrooms:** the colorful image of the white-dotted red mushroom harks back to its hallucinogenic uses in ancient rituals.

- **Money bag:** a self-explanatory image of wealth.

- **Pig:** again, there is a variety of explanations given for why a pig should suggest good luck, but it most probably relates to the enjoyment people experienced eating a pig after it had been fattened up and slaughtered.

- **Horseshoe:** a good luck charm explained by the legend of St. Dunstan shoeing the devil, and folkloric beliefs that such shoes ward off fairies.

- **Champagne:** drinking bubbly wine is a staple of celebrations around the world, but has its origins in France.

- **Liquified lead:** in Germany, the process of melting lead *(blei giessen)* is common at New Year. Small amounts of molten lead are poured into cold water and the meanings of the resulting shapes are interpreted.

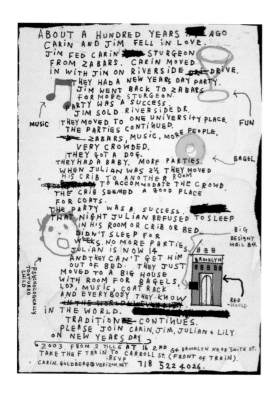

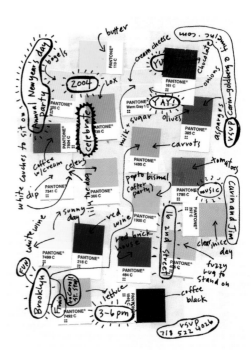

New Year's Party Invitation

★ ★

Design
Carin Goldberg

Client
Self-initiated

Format
Invitations

Country
USA

Carin Goldberg is one of the more prominent graphic designers in the USA, well known in particular for her conceptual and humorous approach to book cover illustrations and record sleeves. For invitations to her own New Year's parties, these same qualities are in evidence. One invitation takes the glass of champagne, one of the most readily identifiable images of New Year celebrations in the West, and presents it in simplified, illustrated form. The other takes Pantone swatches and interprets them in terms of the food and other elements surrounding the celebration.

NATHALIE MELATO   DAVID RONDEL CAMBOU

New Year Greetings

★ ★

Design
Hellohikimori

Client
Self-initiated

Format
Card, e-card

Country
France

Hellohikimori is an exuberant design studio based in Paris, designing for the web and print. Its New Year card for 2007, both printed and online, does a good job of expressing its designer's optimism without engaging in an obvious way with festive iconography.

New Year Gift

★ ★ ★ ★ ★ ★ ★ ★ ★ ★ ★ ★ ★ ★ ★ ★

Studio
Room Corporation

Design and Art Direction
Alexandros Franzolini, Paolo
Prossen, David Mack

Client
Self-initiated

Format
Piggy bank

Country
Italy

While the use of animals is more
associated with the Chinese New
Year, there is also an old European
tradition of using good-luck charms
for the occasion. In Austria and
Germany, and in surrounding
countries such as Italy, the pig is
seen as an emblem of good luck,
and is also the creature that inspired
"piggy banks" for children to save
their pennies. Evoking both these
traditions, this design marks the
New Year 2009 and at the same time
reflects the economic woes of the
moment. It was a corporate gift and
was also made available for purchase
on the design company's website.
"Mr Piggy is an Italian handmade
ceramic piggy bank, coated in gold
plating, with our logo screenprinted
on the back as his tail," explains David
Mack. "Our message is that in 2009,
the best and safest place to put your
money is in your image."

New Year Greetings

★ ★

Studio
Topos Graphics

Design
Seth Labenz, Roy Rub

Client
Self-initiated

Format
Card

Country
USA

The year 2008 was destined to be a momentous year for the USA politically, something that Brooklyn-based designers Topos Graphics wanted to emphasize with their charged New Year's card. Intended to commemorate the forthcoming new government after the elections, its slogan "Out with the old, in with the new" was split in two and printed on alternate sides of heavy paper stock. The color scheme refers both to the stars and stripes of the American flag and the colors of the Republican and Democrat parties.

New Year Greetings

★ ★ ★ ★ ★ ★ ★ ★ ★ ★ ★ ★ ★ ★ ★

Studio
Waterform Design, Inc.

Design
Masayo Nai

Client
Self-initiated

Format
Card

Country
USA

For 2007 and 2008, New York–based designer Masayo Nai sent out these two cards to wish clients and colleagues a Happy New Year. The first card uses the unusual process of photograming (placing objects straight on to photosensitive paper; in effect a photograph without a camera). The kitchen implements seem, at first sight, to be images of festive fireworks or decorations, but on closer inspection they are revealed. The image is printed on silver paper to maximize the contrasts and reversals. The following year's card takes standard party items such as tape and balloons, and transforms them into something equally surreal.

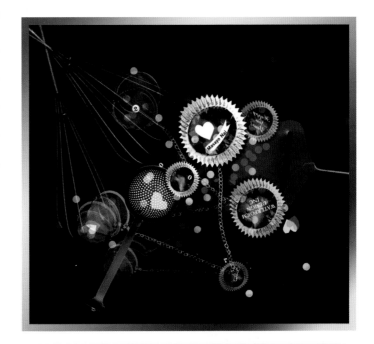

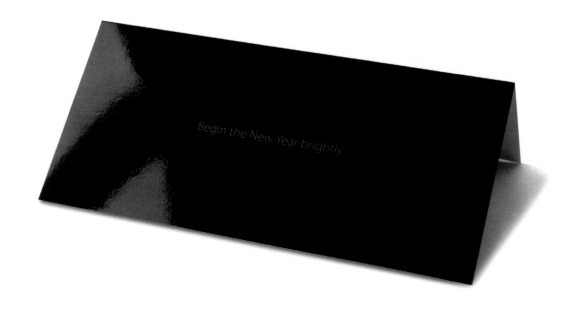

Begin the New Year brightly

New Year Greetings

★ ★

Studio
Curious

Design
Gary Smith, David Baird,
Emma Wilkinson

Art Direction
Gary Smith, Peter Rae

Copywriting
Des Waddy

Illustration
Emma Wilkinson

Client
The Seven Arts Consultancy

Format
Card

Country
UK

The Seven Arts Consultancy, a head-hunting agency for the creative sector, wanted to send a card to its clients and contacts around Europe that would tie in with its branding and catch people's attention. Curious, a London-based design group, was asked to come up with a design, and decided to send a card with a sparkler. The finished card's glossy cover exhorts the recipient to "begin the New Year brightly," and the inside contains the festive sparkler and an illustrated, slightly ironic, step-by-step guide on how to light it.

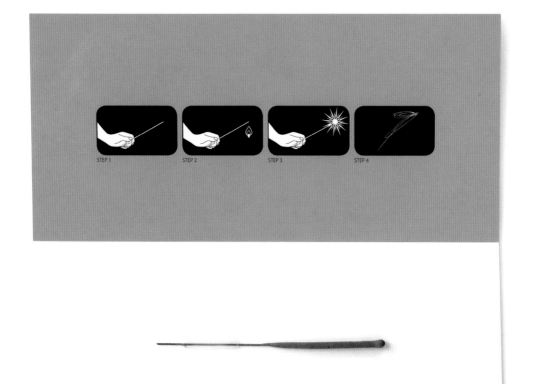

STEP 1   STEP 2   STEP 3   STEP 4

Best wishes for 2009 from Ben and Alison
at The SevenArts Consultancy

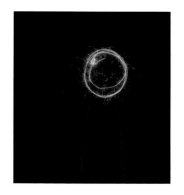 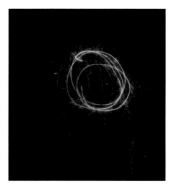 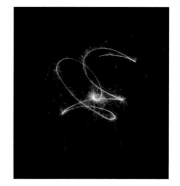

© WU HONG/epa/Corbis

FESTIVAL FACTS

CHINESE NEW YEAR

- Few cultures celebrate the New Year with displays as magnificent as those of China. Traditionally an intricate 15-day celebration, it has been pared down into a simpler celebration, but many colorful features remain.

- Significant expatriate Chinese communities around the world have made the Chinese New Year one of the most recognized festivities and one of the few that is genuinely cross-cultural. In strict observance there are detailed rules as to what is auspicious and will bring good luck.

- The Chinese calendar places the New Year later than the Gregorian calendar; it is celebrated some time between January 21 and February 20, varying year by year.

- The iconography for the Chinese New Year includes the dragon, often seen in the form of lanterns or as costumes worn by a number of people in parade dances. It is a revered, mythological creature believed to ward off evil spirits.

- The Lantern Festival takes place on the 15th day of the Chinese New Year. Lanterns are often decorated with the horoscope animal for the New Year (rat, ox, tiger, rabbit, dragon, snake, horse, ram, monkey, rooster, dog, or pig), and sometimes contain riddles.

- The colors red and gold are regarded as auspicious and are used for a variety of graphics, from the envelopes used to give money to relatives through to cards wishing people good luck.

© Shi Bao Xiu/Redlink/Corbis

Top Left: A Lantern Festival concludes the 15-day celebration of the New Year. Artwork is sometimes showcased in advance, as here at a square in Haiyang, Shandong province, eastern China

Top Right: Red lanterns being hung at Thean Hou Temple in Kuala Lumpur, Malaysia, in advance of the New Year celebrations

Bottom Left: Diamond-shaped cards in the traditional auspicious colors of red and gold, and featuring the character "fu" to wish people good luck are hung indoors and outside

Bottom Right: Lavishly designed red envelopes on a stall at Dihua Market, Taipei, Taiwan. These are used for the giving of money to relatives

Chinese New Year Party Invitation

★ ★

Design
Nicholas Felton

Client
Self-initiated

Format
E-card

Country
USA

Like many designers, Nicholas Felton uses his website and skills for social as well as professional purposes, as in this case when he was holding a party to mark the Chinese New Year in 2007. As this was the Year of the Pig, according to the Chinese calendar, the design he created for his website

and to e-mail to friends was of a pig, but it was an image that evoked pigs in other contexts, such as traditional images of pigs showing the sections taken by butchers.

Chinese New Year Greetings

★ ★

Studio
Shen Design

Design
Juliet Shen

Client
Self-initiated

Format
Card

Country
USA

Every year Juliet Shen, a graphic designer living in Seattle, of Chinese descent, sends out Chinese New Year cards from her studio. The design revolves around the Zodiac animal of the forthcoming year. Shen selects a quote that she thinks is pertinent (sometimes changing it, as for instance, with "the love of monkey"

rather than "the love of money" in the famous saying of Alexis de Tocqueville), before setting it lovingly by hand. Numbered and signed, the images make their recipients pause for thought as they study the intricate typography, and also consider the meaning behind it and the connection between the two cultures.

February

FESTIVAL FACTS

VALENTINE'S DAY

- After Christmas, Valentine's Day accounts for the most cards sold and sent in the world. It is an event that is expressed primarily through graphics. By sending a card (perhaps together with a token gift of chocolates or a rose) to a loved one, the sender either openly or anonymously declares their feelings for the person.

- While this may sound very secular, it is celebrated on February 14, the day in the Roman Catholic calendar when St. Valentine, a Roman martyr, is commemorated. The celebration took hold in Protestant Britain before being exported around the world. Its origins are murky, with theories suggesting it may have its roots in Roman fertility rights or chivalric customs of medieval courtly love.

- The principal image of Valentine's Day is the symbol of love: a heart, usually in red. However, all sorts of images that suggest affection and love—from flowers to puppies—are commonly used.

- While Valentine's Day is celebrated globally, other local festivals celebrate lovers in different ways. For instance, in Brazil the day of lovers (Dia dos Namorados) is celebrated on June 12.

Valentine's Gift

★ ★

Design
EMMI

Client
Self-initiated

Format
Card, badge

Country
UK

This simple Valentine's card plays with the usual format—the card becomes perfunctory and a small attached badge becomes the main item—but its design suggests an envelope containing a message. Slightly mysterious, this design also shows how generalized Valentine's Day has become: rather than a highly charged celebration of a loved one, it is increasingly also an occasion for simply showing goodwill.

Valentine's Greetings

★ ★

Design
Marian Bantjes

Client
Self-initiated

Format
Cards

Country
Canada

Bucking the trend, Canadian designer and illustrator Marian Bantjes sends Valentine and Halloween cards rather than the more usual Christmas or New Year greetings. In 2007 her approach was highly personalized. "I drew 150 hearts and sent one each (personalized, signed, and numbered) to 150 lucky people," she says. The following year the design was very different. "I wrote four fragments of letters; each has no beginning and no end; and each is carefully crafted to hopefully have some resonance with most people," explains Bantjes.

"Each recipient got one fragment. My hope was that they would read the letter several times, and that on the second or third reading they would find something in it for them, something that would make them believe that somehow, through unknown means, I have known something about them all along." The cards, or more properly the folded letter fragments, were hand-written on translucent paper stock.

Stefan

Anni

Jessica

Bill

Ray

Doyald

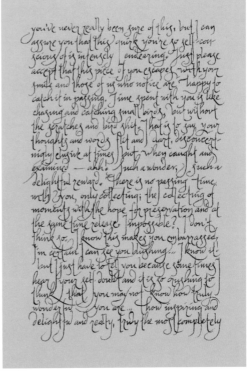

FORM 214-A

2006 VALENTINE INDEX WORKSHEET

TO BE COMPLETED
ON OR BEFORE
FEBRUARY 14, 2006

1. FILING STATUS

Measure your current status by checking all that apply.

		No. of Each	Total
A ☐ Single (Proceed to Section 2)			
B ☐ Dating		_____ x 2	_____
C ☐ In a Relationship		_____ x 3	_____
D ☐ Engaged		_____ x 4	_____
E ☐ Married (or equivalent)		_____ x 5	_____
STATUS INDEX	Add numbers on lines above:		

2. RELATIONSHIP DEDUCTIONS

List any changes in relationship status during the past intra-valentine period.

		No. of Each	Total
A ☐ No Change (Proceed to Section 3)			
B ☐ Stopped Dating....................		_____ x 2	_____
C ☐ Ended Relationship....................		_____ x 3	_____
D ☐ Called off Engagement....................		_____ x 4	_____
E ☐ Divorce (or equivalent)....................		_____ x 5	_____
DEDUCTION INDEX	Add numbers on lines above:		
SUB-TOTAL (may not be less than 0)....................	Subtract above from section 1 total		

3. CRUSH CREDITS

For credit purposes, crushes are restricted to individuals who know your name, and restricted to 5 persons. One credit per person.

YOUR CRUSHES

1 _____
2 _____
3 _____
4 _____
5 _____

CRUSHES ON YOU

1 _____
2 _____
3 _____
4 _____
5 _____

Total crush credits: ☐

4. ADJUSTED VALENTINE INDEX

Carry this total to reverse.

Combine totals from Section 2 and 3, this is your **Adjusted Valentine Index** ☐

WORKSHEET © 2006 NICHOLAS FELTON / FELTRON.COM

Valentine's Greetings

★ ★ ★ ★ ★ ★ ★ ★ ★ ★ ★ ★ ★ ★ ★

Design
Nicholas Felton

Client
Self-initiated

Format
E-card

Country
USA

Not everyone welcomes Valentine's Day. This design by New York–based Nicholas Felton casts a wry, cynical eye over the affair. Rather than draw on the stock imagery of love and use hearts, cherubs, or flowers, he notes its proximity to US tax deadlines and humorously presents the information in the manner of a bureaucratic form to be filled in.

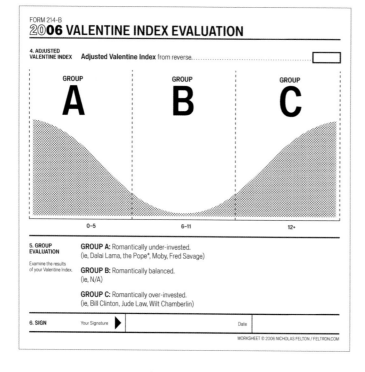

FORM 214-B

2006 VALENTINE INDEX EVALUATION

4. ADJUSTED VALENTINE INDEX Adjusted Valentine Index from reverse.................... ☐

GROUP
A

GROUP
B

GROUP
C

0–5   6–11   12+

5. GROUP EVALUATION

Examine the results of your Valentine Index.

GROUP A: Romantically under-invested.
(ie, Dalai Lama, the Pope*, Moby, Fred Savage)

GROUP B: Romantically balanced.
(ie, N/A)

GROUP C: Romantically over-invested.
(ie, Bill Clinton, Jude Law, Wilt Chamberlin)

6. SIGN Your Signature ▶ _____   Date _____

WORKSHEET © 2006 NICHOLAS FELTON / FELTRON.COM

Valentine's Greetings

★ ★

Design

Rob Ryan

Client

Self-initiated

Format

Card

Country

UK

A Valentine's card, however lovely, is usually a rather ephemeral thing. But Rob Ryan, a British paper-cutting artist, hit upon the idea of creating a Valentine card that was a limited-edition, screenprinted, and signed artwork—something enduring, like the love that is professed.

Valentine's Day Campaign

★ ★

Studio
Kolegram

Art Direction
Jean Luc Denat

Client
Self-initiated

Format
Poster

Country
Canada

Valentine's cards are usually personal and rather discreet affairs, but the designers at Kolegram, based in Gatineau, Canada, decided they would mark the occasion in a different way, by creating what they describe as "a viral campaign throughout the city to celebrate the day and spread love." Partnering with outdoor media company Diffusart, their humorous yet serious posters were pasted over the city. The images generated a strong response, with people calling up to request posters and the designers being interviewed on the radio to explain what they had done.

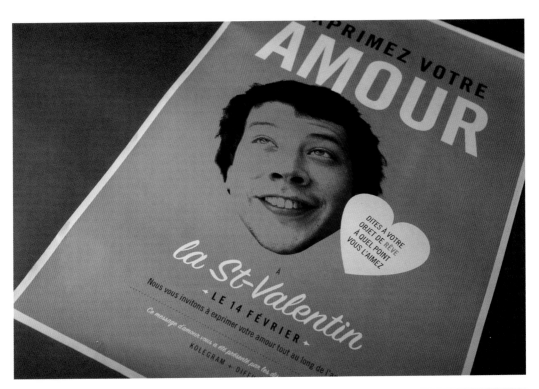

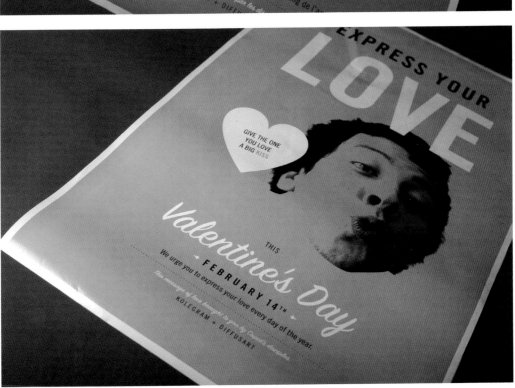

DESIGN TIMES SQUARE
DAVID SLATOFF

TIMES SQUARE ALLIANCE

DESIGN TIMES SQUARE
CHIP WASS

TIMES SQUARE ALLIANCE

DESIGN TIMES SQUARE
RODRIGO CORRAL

TIMES SQUARE ALLIANCE

Valentine's Day Campaign

★ ★

Design
Various, coordinated by Mark
Randall at World Studio Inc.

Client
Times Square Alliance

Format
Banners

Country
USA

In 2009, building on a successful event the previous year, the street furniture of Manhattan was co-opted to display Valentine's Day imagery by 12 different graphic designers. The project, Love in Times Square, saw the designers treat the word "love" in very different ways, with the resulting designs hung on banners in and around Times Square. Rather than a specific personalized message of love or a commercial push to buy merchandise, the intention was to create an intervention that would suggest a more generalized atmosphere of peace, enchantment, and goodwill. The designers involved were Marian Bantjes, Rodrigo Corral, John Fulbrook, Goodesign, Carin Goldberg, Number 17, Paul Sahre, David Slatoff, James Victore, Chip Wass, and Worldstudio.

DESIGN TIMES SQUARE
GOODESIGN

DESIGN TIMES SQUARE
JAMES VICTORE

DESIGN TIMES SQUARE
WORLDSTUDIO

Photo by Emile Wamsteker

© Richard Cummins/Corbis

© SERGIO MORAES/Reuters/Corbis

- Carnival, probably the most exuberant of all festivals, derives from the last chance to party and indulge before the austerities of the Christian period of Lent. It has become one of the biggest reasons to party globally.

- *Carnevale,* as it is known in Italian, means "goodbye to meat or flesh."

- The day before Lent is known as Shrove Tuesday, Pancake Day, or Fat Tuesday, which is *mardi gras* in French, and it is this name by which the carnival events in many cities, including New Orleans and Sydney, are known. While these and Rio de Janeiro's carnival, the most overwhelming of them all, are some of the biggest events in the international calendar, other carnivals around the world are also major events, particularly those in Trinidad, and Tenerife in the Canary Islands.

- Images of abundance, typically of tropical fruit or plumage, abound, as do sensual images of semi-nudity. Carnival is an excuse to dress up, often in fancy costumes or masks, and is all about breaking stifling conventions. Anything goes as long as it is visually arresting.

Top: An array of traditional Carnevale masks for sale in Venice

Bottom: A dancer, in characteristically extravagant costume, taking part in the second night of parades at the Sambadrome in Rio de Janeiro, 2006. This dancer is part of the Viradouro Samba School

Right: A typically voluptuous carnival graphic, this 1937 poster for Carnival in Panama is signed Artes Graphicas, "Senefelder," Ecuador

Sydney Gay and Lesbian Mardi Gras Poster

★ ★

Design

Lewis Oswald

Art Direction

Damien Eames

Photography

Helen White

Client

Self-initiated

Format

Poster

Country

Australia

In 2009 the organizers of the Sydney Gay and Lesbian Mardi Gras decided that the theme for the main parade, which is the focus or "jewel in the crown" of the event, should be "nations united." For the official poster and graphic identity, designed in-house, a variety of multicultural models, in various scanty costumes, were photographed and montaged into a deliberately and conspicuously Photoshopped image. The two logos for the event (one derived from an orb, the other from the Sydney Opera House) are both prominent, but subservient to the Rainbow flag, which is the main icon of gay solidarity and diversity.

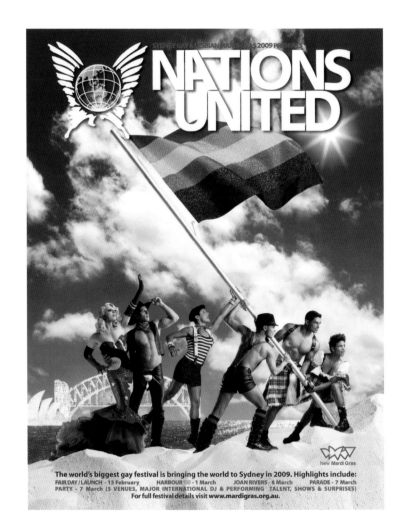

Vida 10.0

X ANIVERSARIO VIDA
CONCURSO INTERNACIONAL
ARTE Y VIDA ARTIFICIAL

10TH ANNIVERSARY VIDA
INTERNATIONAL COMPETITION
ON ART AND ARTIFICIAL LIFE

Vida 10.0 Invitation

★ ★

Studio
Erretres

Design and Art Direction
Daniel Barrios, Pablo Rubio

Client
Telefónica

Format
Invitation

Country
Spain

For a technology festival, Vida 10.0, held in in Barcelona, Madrid-based graphic design group Erretres came up with the idea of an invitation that would mimic a motherboard. The idea was that the chips and circuitry would be totally integrated with the logo and typography. This design was married up with an advertising campaign and a website. The heart of the festival is a competition to reward the best project uniting artistic creativity and artificial intelligence.

March

1st: St. David's Day (p 043)

8th: International Women's Day (p 042)

Budapest Spring Festival – arts festival, Budapest, Hungary

La Noche de los Teatros (pp 044–045)

La Noche de los Libros (pp 044–045)

Polynesian Pasifika Festival – cultural festival, Auckland, New Zealand

Las Fallas – saint's day (St. Joseph), Valencia, Spain

17th: St. Patrick's Day (pp 046–047)

Figures of Speech Gala (pp 040–041)

Last week: Lord of the Tremors – religious thanksgiving festival, Cusco, Peru

Semana Santa – Easter Holy Week celebrations, Antigua, Guatemala; Avila, Spain

Holi (pp 048–049)

Easter (pp 050–057)

Figures of Speech Gala Invitation

* *

Design
Sarah Boris

Client
Institute of Contemporary
Arts (ICA), London

Format
Invitation

Country
UK

In March 2008, the Institute of Contemporary Arts in London organized its first Figures of Speech gala—a fundraising event celebrating freedom of speech—with a series of celebrities introducing and talking about one object they could not live without. Sarah Boris designed the invitation for the inaugural event as well as that for the following year. "Speech is represented by a clear speech bubble in the center," she explains. "The speech bubble is empty to convey the idea that what will be said is uncontrolled and free. As the invitations were sent to a high-profile audience, the brief required a glamorous, luxurious, and contemporary feel, hence the use of fine gold foiling on thick, uncoated card. The card is square and very bulky for maximum impact."

Kurdish women hold placards at a
parade for International Women's Day
in Istanbul, Turkey, March 8, 2009

FESTIVAL FACTS

**INTERNATIONAL
WOMEN'S DAY
AND WOMEN'S
HISTORY MONTH**

- International Women's Day has its origins in the fight
  for universal suffrage at the beginning of the twentieth
  century, and has maintained a political, campaigning
  edge despite being celebrated initially on different days.

- Today, March 8 is the accepted date, and the event
  is supported by a variety of governments around the
  world and promoted by the United Nations.

- Women's History Month is a more loosely structured
  occasion. In the USA and in some other countries,
  it is celebrated in March as an event surrounding
  International Women's Day. However, in Canada it
  is celebrated in October.

St. David's Day Campaign

★ ★

Design
Elfen

Client
S4C

Format
Card, viral e-mail,
television promos, T-shirts

Country
Wales

St. David is the patron saint of Wales and every year, on March 1, the country celebrates its national day with parades and concerts. While it is not an official public holiday, St. David's Day is widely celebrated, and people often wear leeks and daffodils, the two symbols of Wales and St. David, respectively. S4C is a Welsh TV channel that broadcasts primarily in the Welsh language or with Welsh subtitling. It commissioned Cardiff-based designers Elfen to develop a campaign to stimulate interest in its festival-related programming, including a card that was mailed out to every Welsh home in the UK. In addition there was an e-mail campaign that asked viewers to identify icons as Welsh, or not; a similar TV campaign; and T-shirts emblazoned with the design.

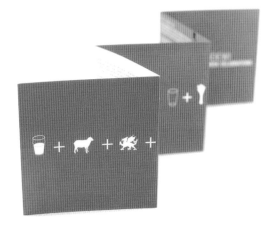

La Noche de los Teatros and La Noche de Los Libros Identities

★ ★ ★ ★ ★ ★ ★ ★ ★ ★ ★ ★ ★ ★ ★

Studio
Erretres

Design
Daniel Barrios, Gema Navarro,
Wiebke Harzer

Client
Comunidad de Madrid
(Madrid's local government)

Format
Logo

Country
Spain

In 2007, the Spanish capital Madrid
hosted two linked cultural festivals,
La Noche de los Teatros (The Night
of Theater) in March, and La Noche
de Los Libros (The Night of Books),
held in April. The designers devised
an identity consisting of two circles,
one containing the logo and date of
the event, the other a photograph
of a full moon. This flexible imagery
was used in many applications, from
balloons and brochures through to
advertising, signage, and bags, all of
which made the whole city aware
of what was going on. The designers
say they wanted Madrid to seem
temporarily "invaded by the identity."

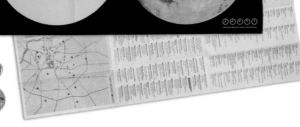

FESTIVAL FACTS

ST. PATRICK'S DAY

Children dressed in typical attire for a St. Patrick's Day celebration in Birmingham, England

- It is commonly noted that St. Patrick's Day is one of the only national days to be celebrated by other countries, and for that one day many non-Irish people choose to become Irish, or what they think is Irish.

- The festival marks the feast day of St. Patrick, the patron saint of Ireland, who, according to legend, chased the snakes from the island.

- While the Irish capital of Dublin hosts a very large five-day celebration, this is dwarfed by the even larger St. Patrick's Parade in Manhattan, and there are extensive celebrations in many other cities around the world.

- The iconography comprises the shamrock, a three-leaf clover allegedly used by St. Patrick to explain the Catholic concept of the Trinity and now the national emblem of Ireland. Green is the national color of Ireland, as a result of the adoption of the shamrock. In the USA in particular it is customary to mark the day by wearing green items of clothing. In Chicago the River Chicago is dyed green for the occasion, as are various other rivers in the USA. Other common images seen as typically Irish are the Irish harp and the leprechaun, a small mythical figure, often depicted wearing a tall hat which is recreated and worn by people participating in St. Patrick's Day events.

GREEN
IS THE
THEME!
MONDAY
MARCH 17th
JOIN CULTURE SHOCK IN CELEBRATING
SAINT PATRICK'S DAY 2008

St. Patrick's Day Promotion

★ ★ ★ ★ ★ ★ ★ ★ ★ ★ ★ ★ ★ ★ ★

Design
Jason Bolton

Client
Oden's Culture Shock

Format
Poster

Country
USA

Often festive graphics serve a straightforward purpose, as in this unpretentious poster reminding people working for Oden to dress in green and celebrate St. Patrick's Day on March 17. Printed on an inkjet printer, it simply presents the two main elements of the festivity: the color green and the shamrock.

FESTIVAL FACTS

HOLI

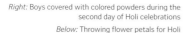

Right: Boys covered with colored powders during the
second day of Holi celebrations

Below: Throwing flower petals for Holi

@ Mbostock/flickr

- There can be few more visual festivals than Holi, even by the colorful standards of the Hindu religion. Holi, the festival of color, is celebrated in the north of India and in neighboring Nepal. It is essentially a spring festival, celebrated for three days around the full moon in the month of Phalguna in the Hindu calendar (February 20 to March 20 in the Gregorian calendar).

- Holi has ancient origins that have merged with Hindu myths, in particular the burning of the female demon Holika. This lives on in the bonfires that are lit to celebrate this exuberant event, which is also accompanied by the drinking of alcohol and the consumption of hallucinogenics.

- Holi's main feature comes on the second day when there is an anarchic throwing of colored water, powder pigments, or mud, covering all participants including bystanders, whether willing or unwilling. Indeed, so raucous is the festival that there are now health campaigns seeking to protect participants from unpleasant repercussions due to contact with the modern, sometimes toxic pigments that have taken the place of older, natural preparations.

FESTIVAL FACTS

EASTER

- Easter is the most important event in the Christian calendar despite being overshadowed by Christmas in most Christian countries. It marks the Crucifixion and Resurrection of Jesus Christ. The week leading up to Easter, known as Holy Week, commemorates the last days of Jesus Christ, including Palm Sunday (Jesus's entry to Jerusalem), Maundy Thursday (the Last Supper), and Good Friday, the day on which he was crucified. Easter itself starts on the Sunday, when he was resurrected. The festivities are accompanied by a variety of liturgical events depending on the denomination.

- Easter has no fixed date, something that, historically, has attracted controversy and periodic attempts at rationalization, all of which have been in vain. Western Christianity celebrates Easter between March 22 and April 25 according to the Gregorian calendar, while Eastern Christianity celebrates it between those same dates according to the Julian calendar. The precise date is set according to computations relating to a lunisolar calendar.

- Centuries of Christian art have resulted in a highly detailed iconography for the Passion of Christ and Easter. The images of the crucifixion and the crucifix itself endure, but this more complex imagery is now largely the preserve of the art gallery or Church.

- Nonreligious elements are also a strong part of Easter celebrations, and tend to be more common in contemporary graphics for Easter. These incorporate ancient spring rites, most notably the Easter egg, a symbol of rebirth. Older traditions of hand-decorating actual eggs are being supplanted by gift eggs produced by chocolate manufacturers, usually in ornate or themed packaging. One tradition has the eggs being hidden by the Easter bunny to be discovered by children. Bunnies and chicks, common Easter graphics, are both symbols of fertility, birth, and spring. Other common symbols are essentially spring images, such as flowers and branches in bud.

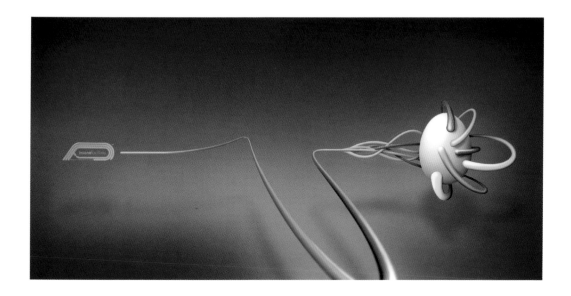

Easter Gift

★ ★

Studio
InsaneFacilities

Design
Jarek Berecki

Client
Self-initiated

Format
Digital wallpaper

Country
Poland

Like so many designers, Jarek Berecki, who is based in Lodz in Poland, wanted to use a festive occasion to build on his relationships with friends and clients. For Easter 2008 he decided to create a wallpaper design that could be sent or downloaded from his website instead of the more usual printed card. "I tried to design something different. It was a kind of experiment," he says. He played with color and perspective, but underneath the image the Easter egg, and the central European tradition of painting boiled eggs, remains clearly identifiable.

Easter Campaign

★ ★

Design
Rob Ryan

Client
Fortnum & Mason

Format
Packaging

Country
UK

Exclusive London retailer Fortnum & Mason specializes in festive food and hampers that are exquisitely packaged, either in a very traditional manner or by employing contemporary talents, as it did for its 2009 Easter egg range. This packaging was designed by Rob Ryan, an illustrator and designer well known for his delicate die cuts. Here his die-cut technique is rendered illustratively on the outer sleeves that envelop the boxes containing the festive chocolate eggs.

Easter Campaign

★ ★

Studio
Irving Designs

Design and Art Direction
Lucia Giaggiotti,
Julian Roberts

Client
Carluccio's

Format
Packaging

Country
UK

Carluccio's is a chain of Italian stores, delicatessens, and restaurants in the UK started by celebrity chef Antonio Carluccio. The stores regularly run promotions connected with various festivals, including Easter, always with a distinctly Italian flavor. In Catholic Italy, Easter is one of the most important occasions of the year. *Buona Pasqua* translates as "Happy Easter." As is so often the case, food is a main ingredient of the festival. *Colomba*, a dove-shaped cake made with butter, eggs, and candied orange peel, is traditionally served with a glass of dessert wine during Easter week. These designs by Irving for the 2007 and 2008 seasons evoke traditional Italian packaging.

Easter Campaign

★ ★

Studio
Room Corporation

Design
Paolo Prossen, David Mack

Client
Lindt & Sprüngli

Format
Packaging

Country
Italy

Come Easter, chocolate makers across Europe vie for attention with enticing packaging for their seasonal products, in particular their large chocolate eggs. Like those of so many chocolate producers, these designs for famous Swiss brand Lindt & Sprüngli are aimed principally at the youth market,

predominantly children. They were created specifically for the Italian market by Milanese design group Room Corporation. In 2006, a new chocolate product aimed at adults was introduced. Flavored with red chili pepper, it was adorned with a "passionate" flamed design.

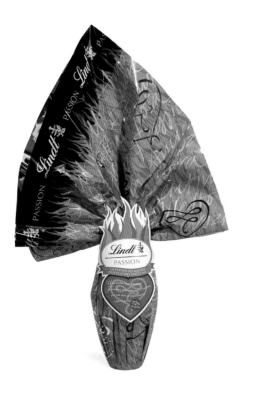

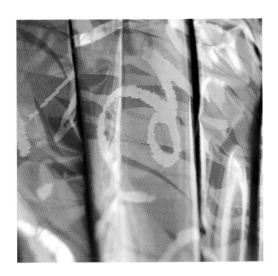

Weddings

Turkish/US Wedding

★ ★

Design
Burak Karavit

Client
Isenbike Ordu, Kenan Ordu

Format
Invitation

Country
Turkey/USA

When two close friends of designer Burak Karavit decided to get married, he came up with a concept for a wedding invitation that would act as a little narrative about how the couple met and where they were going to get married. A "photo story," slightly reminiscent of teenage magazines, relates how the couple met in New York and were going to get married in Istanbul in Turkey. This "film strip" is viewed as the insert is pulled out

and seen through a die-cut hole in the outer, matte black casing. A monogram combining the couple's initials is also foil-printed in silver on this casing. As the invitations were going to be distributed by hand and didn't require envelopes, this unusual approach was more practical than it would otherwise have been.

Fall Wedding

★ ★ ★ ★ ★ ★ ★ ★ ★ ★ ★ ★ ★ ★ ★

Studio
nothingdiluted

Design
Grant Dickson

Client
Jayne Walker, Steven Walker

Format
Stationery

Country
UK

Seasonal colors were the inspiration for this stationery for a sumptuous wedding held in the fall, in Northern Ireland. To capture the "tones and textures" of fall foliage, designer Grant Dickson chose a two-color print process including a gold-colored ink. As well as an ornate logo joining the bride and bridegroom's initials, a sans serif font assisted in creating a look that suggested all the luxury of a grand traditional wedding, but expressed in more contemporary aesthetic terms. The wedding stationery consisted of A6 [105 × 148mm (c. 4 × 5³/₄in)] day and evening cards, printed envelopes, menus, table settings, and thank-you cards, all printed on the same quality paper stock.

Jeff Fisher & Ed Cunningham

Gay Wedding

★ ★

Studio
LogoMotives

Design
Jeff Fisher

Client
Self-initiated

Format
E-card, invitations, signage,
thank-you notes

Country
USA

Gay marriage has been controversial
in the USA, but designer Jeff Fisher
took advantage of a period when
the practice was permitted in his
state of Oregon to marry his partner
Ed Cunningham. As a designer
specializing in logo design and
corporate identity, he naturally chose
to devise a logo for the event that

could be used in a variety of ways
and that would encapsulate their
respective personalities. "The
simplified graphics of the logo
represented my partner and I well.
He's the business type, managing
a corporate law firm office, while
I'm the creative type, often wearing
Hawaiian-style shirts," he says.

Hawaiian Wedding

★ ★

Studio
Cowley Design

Design
Sara Cowley

Client
Anna Costello, Seth Costello

Format
Stationery

Country
USA

"This wedding invitation set was designed for a couple who were married in Hawaii, but hosted a celebration for those who were unable to attend. The couple are from the South, but now reside in California, so this stationery set was meant to reflect a Southern hospitality vibe," explains Sara Cowley, who created the work for these long-standing clients.

"A handwriting typeface was used to create a personal feeling, along with pastel illustrations. The 'peach' color was inspired by the state fruit of Georgia. The couple wanted the event to have an intimate, 'dinner with friends' kind of feeling, and these elements helped in creating that."

Irish Wedding

★ ★ ★ ★ ★ ★ ★ ★ ★ ★ ★ ★ ★ ★ ★

Studio
wemakedesign

Design
Nik Dillon

Illustration
Adam Gallacher

Client
Suzanne Lynam, Eoin Lynam

Format
Stationery

Country
Ireland

A sister and bridesmaid of the bride, Dublin-based designer Nik Dillon wanted to create wedding stationery that would be an enduring gift. The couple had got engaged in Miami and their brief was just to "bring Miami to the stationery." Together with illustrator Adam Gallacher, Nik developed a design that evoked the architecture and colors of Miami art deco. A full suite of stationery was designed around this theme, including invitations, place names, reply cards, thank-you cards, a wedding list, wedding Mass booklets, and information cards. While the wedding was traditional in format, Dillon hoped that the stationery would be "contemporary, stylish, and memorable."

SUZANNE & EOIN

SUZANNE & EOIN
WOULD BE DELIGHTED IF

_____

COULD JOIN THEM ON THE OCCASION
OF THEIR MARRIAGE IN
THE CHURCH OF THE SACRED HEART
AUGHRIM, CO. WICKLOW
AT 1.30pm ON THURSDAY, OCTOBER 2nd, 2008.

FOLLOWED BY A RECEPTION AND PARTY IN
THE BROOKLODGE AND WELLS SPA
MACREDDIN VILLAGE, AUGHRIM, CO. WICKLOW

RSVP
September 1st, 2008
49 Priory Way
Manor Grove
Terenure
Dublin 12

DRESS CODE
Ladies: Cocktail Attire
Men: Jacket & Tie
Shoes: Dancing!

Don't Wait!
Reply by September 1st

_____

☐ YES, WOULDN'T MISS IT!

☐ SORRY, CAN'T MAKE IT.

SPECIAL DIETARY REQUIREMENTS, PLEASE LET US KNOW.

WEDDING GIFT LIST

Celebrate with Trailfinders

TRAILFINDERS
THE TRAVEL EXPERTS

DIRECTIONS & INFO

DUBLIN
DUN LAOGHAIRE
BRAY
ENNISKERRY
GREYSTONES
DELGANY
KILKOOLE
NEWTOWNMOUNTKENNEDY
NEWCASTLE
ROUNDWOOD
GLENDALOUGH
ASHFORD
RATHNEW
WICKLOW
RATHDRUM
AGHAVANNAGH
★ BROOKLODGE & WELLS SPA
MACREDDIN
AUGHRIM
AVOCA
WOODENBRIDGE
ARKLOW

Come fly with me!
Let's fly, let's fly, let's fly...

A GIFT LIST IS HELD AT TRAILFINDERS FOR SUZANNE DILLON & EOIN LYNAM'S WEDDING ON 2ND OCTOBER 2008

PLEASE QUOTE THE GIFT LIST REFERENCE WHEN YOU MAKE A CONTRIBUTION:

GIFT LIST REFERENCE: RA83YM
CLOSING DATE: 12TH OCTOBER 2008

This Gift List has been opened as a unique way to help you contribute towards a trip of a lifetime for family and friends. Available in denominations of €5's, there is a minimum contribution of €20.

Please include any special message you would like us to convey, which will be forwarded with your contribution when the gift closes. An acknowledgement of your payment will be sent you. The Wedding Gift List will be closed on the date stated above and it will not be possible to process any further payments after this date.

Making a contribution could not be simpler:

➤ Visit our website www.trailfinders.ie, follow the links to our Wedding & Gift List and enter your Visa or Mastercard. 24 hours a day, 7 days a week.

➤ Call 01 881 4950 with details of your Visa, Mastercard, Amex, Diners or Laser (€1500 daily limit per card). Mon to Sat 9am – 6pm, Sun 10am – 6pm.

➤ Visit our Dublin or Cork Travel Centres: 4/5 Dawson St, Dublin 2 or 40/41 Marlboro St, Cork. Cheques, Cash, Visa, Mastercard, Amex, Diners, Maestro, Draft or Laser (€1500 daily limit per card) are accepted.

➤ Send a cheque to Trailfinders Wedding & Gift List Service, 4/5 Dawson St, Dublin 2. Please make cheques payable to Trailfinders Ltd and write the name of the recipient, their Gift List Reference, the date of the special occasion, your address and a contact telephone number on the back of the cheque. Please allow 10 working days prior to the closing date for cheque clearance. Foreign currency cheques are not acceptable.

Philippine Wedding

★ ★

Design
ElectroLychee

Client
Patricia Marcelo,
Adrian Magbanua

Format
Postcards

Country
The Philippines

Looking for something a bit different, a couple who refer to themselves simply as Pat and Ian approached Manila-based illustration and design agency ElectroLychee to design their wedding invitations. While it was a grand wedding, they wanted something that wasn't stuffy and traditional, and that would reflect their mutual interests, such as music and travel, and their "baby"—a classic Volkswagen car called Lucille.

The result was a set of funky, illustrated postcards, with all the relevant practical information associated with a big wedding, such as attire, wedding lists, RSVP requests and so on, relegated to the flip side. The copywriting mirrors the visual style, referring to the wedding as the "exchange of I Do."

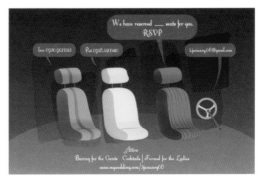

Indian Wedding

* *

Studio
UMS Design Studio

Art Direction
Ulhas Moses

Design, Paper Engineering,
and Illustration
Siddharth Kulkarni

Client
POP-U-LOVE cards

Format
Card

Country
India

There are few countries that celebrate weddings more elaborately or with more enthusiasm than India. While traditional Hindu weddings can last up to five days, more modern occasions are often considerably abbreviated. Either way, central to Hindu wedding ritual is the sacred fire, or *Agni*, which has to be circled seven times by the bride and bridegroom. The actual fireplace is the *Agnikund*, which is recreated in these wedding cards created

by Mumbai-based UMS Design Studio. Opening the hard-backed card reveals the *Agnikund* as a paper-engineered pop-up, which the designers intend as a very literal invitation to participate in the ceremony. The gold coloring of the card further reinforces the fire reference, and is used not only for the card, but for printing the ornate traditional patterning, as well as for the typography, which is gold foil stamped.

British Indian Wedding

★ ★ ★ ★ ★ ★ ★ ★ ★ ★ ★ ★ ★ ★

Design

Creative ID

Client

Magna Shah

Format

Invitation

Country

UK

"The bride, a British Asian, wanted an invitation that looked elegant and sophisticated. It needed to incorporate Indian elements, yet look contemporary," explains Vaishali Shah of Creative ID in London. "We chose traditional Indian colors of bright pink and orange, and then added turquoise to make it look more contemporary. We used an abstract, modern version of the lotus, a sacred flower in India, as the icon to run across all the stationery. We also incorporated a henna pattern as part of the design, which was used on the inside of the main envelope as well as on the inside of the wedding folder." Metallic board was chosen for its "festive shimmer," and also because it would act as a good background for the strong colors of the design, which was hand embellished with diamantés as a finishing touch. The client liked the invitation so much that she commissioned a suite of stationery in the same vein for the wedding ceremony and reception.

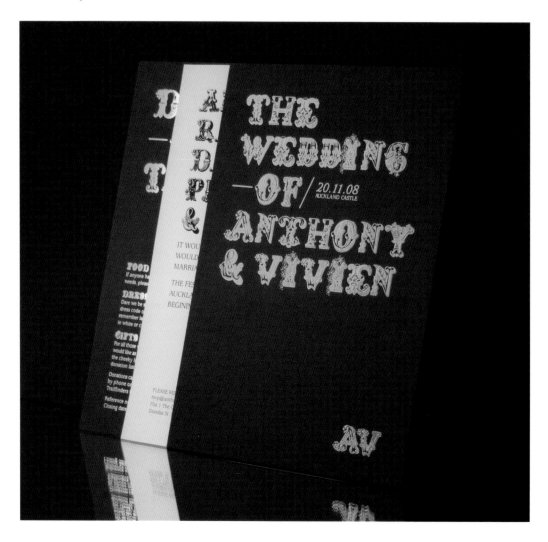

English Wedding

★ ★

Design
Blue River Design

Client
Anthony Cantwell,
Vivien Hedges

Format
Invitation

Country
UK

When designer Anthony Cantwell got married and designed his own wedding invitations, he decided to create something modern and different rather than the standard traditional fare. Looking instead like a cabaret invite, they were printed on black (rather than white) card, with highly ornate nineteenth-century typography picked out in gold. Included in the envelope (which was fixed with black sealing wax) was a separate insert on white stock, personalized to the invitee.

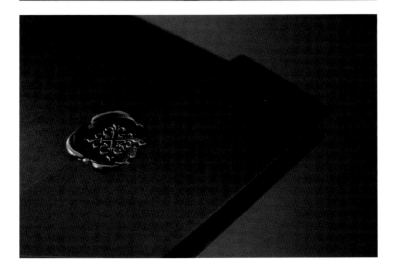

Spanish Wedding

★ ★

Design
Carol García del Busto

Client
Rafa Capuz Bacete,
Cristiana Zamorano García;
Patricia Madrid Saus,
Juan Carlos Benet Vicedo

Format
Invitations

Country
Spain

For these two simple wedding invitations, Spanish designer Carol García del Busto picked up on characteristic features of these friends and made them the main features of the designs. Rafa Capuz Bacete and Cristiana Zamorano García are fond of playing card games, so the imagery of traditional card designs was plundered to create the King and Queen of Hearts. The flower the queen holds is developed into a little motif to grace the front of the invitation.

Patricia Madrid Saus and Juan Carlos Benet Vicedo are traditional in their outlook, which the designer picked up on by presenting classical nineteenth-century Spanish wedding costumes, but giving them a little twist by presenting them as old-fashioned children's illustrations to be cut out and put on a paper mannequin.

Rafa Capuz Bacete
y
Cristina Zamorano García

Se complacen en invitarle a la ceremonia de su boda
que se celebrará el día 8 de marzo a las 18 horas
en la Iglesia Colegial Basílica de Santa María (La Seu)

Y a la cena que se servirá
a continuación en los
Salones Reina de Xàtiva

Xàtiva, 2008

Teléfono: 654 513 417 · Nº de invitados: ___
Se ruega se comunique la no asistencia

Canadian Wedding

★ ★ ★ ★ ★ ★ ★ ★ ★ ★ ★ ★ ★ ★

Studio
AmoebaCorp

Design
Mikey Richardson

Client
Self-initiated

Format
Invitation

Country
Canada

In 2006, Canadian designer Mikey Richardson married Sandi Gidluck. While both live in Toronto, in the east of Canada, the wedding was taking place in the west, in the foothills of Alberta where the bride grew up. This long trip west inspired a theme of "East meets West" and a nostalgic "old Western" aesthetic that was used for the wedding graphics, which primarily consisted of a 12-page travel guide. This provided guests with basic information about the wedding and about the area it was being held in, with details of accommodation and visitor attractions, as well as maps. It was printed on very pulpy uncoated stock and stitched together with thread. A variety of retro fonts and flourishes enhanced the effect. "To play into the kitschy side of travel, we also sent out a 'save the date' Western-themed fridge magnet, the kind you would find and collect when you travel," says Richardson.

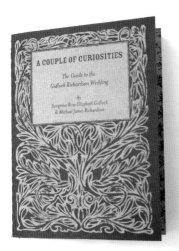

Chinese Wedding ‹

★ ★ ★ ★ ★ ★ ★ ★ ★ ★ ★ ★ ★ ★ ★

Design
Winnie Li

Client
Maria Lam, Francis Chan

Format
Invitation

Country
USA

When California-based Winnie Li was asked by a friend to design an invitation for her wedding in California, she wanted something that would reflect her Chinese roots and yet incorporate Western aspects. Li decided on a traditionally Chinese palette of red (matte ink) and gold (glossy ink) and combined that with a more Western approach to typography. The overall concept was influenced by the Chinese festive tradition of paper cutouts on windows and walls. The design was printed on glassine to suggest a similar fragility and delicacy. The invitation was sent out to its lucky recipients as a poster.

Spanish/English Wedding ›

★ ★

Design
Rob Ryan

Client
Alicia and Michael

Format
Invitation

Country
UK

The delicate paper-cut works of British artist Rob Ryan have been in demand for weddings, including, on one occasion, being translated into the lace elements of a wedding dress. Of this invitation Ryan says, "Alicia and Michael asked me to do the wedding invitation and the whole thing was a total pleasure and a lot of fun to boot. It was great getting them on it too, mainly because they are both so beautiful, but also because Michael has nice long legs that are nice to draw. It was cool having the words in both English and Spanish too."

English Wedding

★ ★

Studio
Planet Interactive Arts

Design and Art Direction
Bobbie Haslett, Phil Bradwick

Client
Timothy Clacy, Emily Leyden

Format
Invitation, table plan,
table names, menu

Country
UK

As the couple getting married initially met at a music festival, and going to such festivals continued to be their mutual passion, they asked that the designs for their wedding invitation should be themed around this. The wedding itself was going to mimic a music festival—held in a barn, it was to feature live music performed in tents. "The invitations were based on festival tickets, right down to the barcode, which changed depending on whether people were invited to the wedding or just the reception," says designer Bobbie Haslett. These went down so well with the couple that they then asked for other materials to be designed for the wedding. The table plan, for instance, was designed around the kind of festival map found at most UK festivals, with colored tents representing tables.

MENU

STARTER
Sweet potato soup, with basil oil & croutons

MAIN COURSE
Rack of lamb with roasted potatoes and vegetables

Vegetarian Option – Five bean & potato ragout

DESERT
Sticky toffee pudding served with ice cream

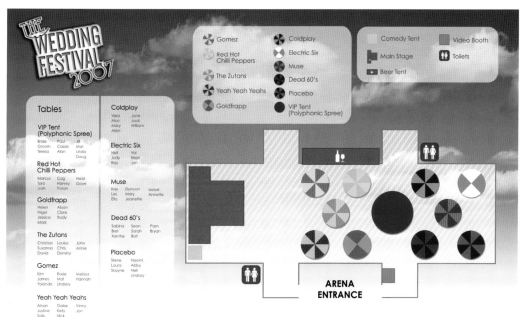

Hindu Wedding

★ ★ ★ ★ ★ ★ ★ ★ ★ ★ ★ ★ ★ ★ ★

Design
Neha Motipara

Client
Self-initiated

Format
Champagne card, organza
bag, cello envelope

Country
USA

Hindu weddings are often extensive
affairs, including that of New Jersey
designer Neha Motipara. She designed
her own stationery to function for six
separate events over three days. The
color scheme reflected the sari she
would wear and the Hindu belief
that the color red brings good luck.
As there were four event cards as
well as a card with a map and
directions, reply cards, and a
stamped envelope, she decided to
create a pouch in which these could
all be placed. The pouch, also in red,
was then placed in a transparent cello
wrapper to allow for posting. The
cards themselves were cut by hand
and decorated with mini Swarovski
crystals "to provide some glitz."

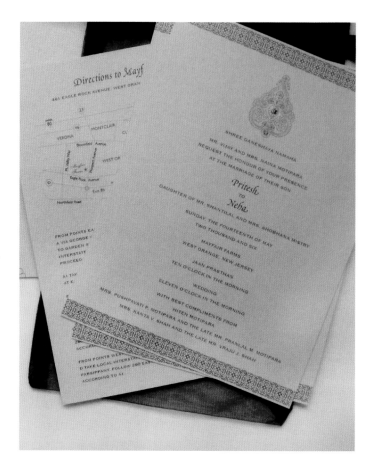

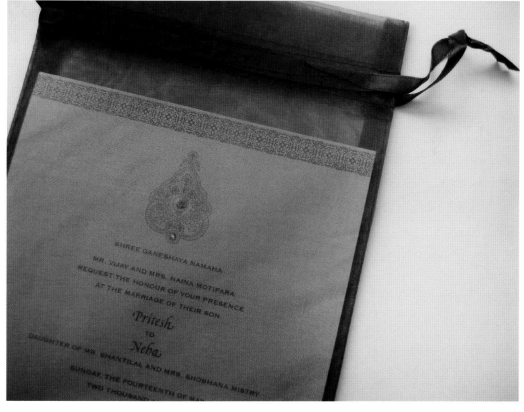

SHREE GANESHAYA NAMAHA

MR. VIJAY AND MRS. NAINA MOTIPARA
REQUEST THE HONOUR OF YOUR PRESENCE
AT THE MARRIAGE OF THEIR SON

Pritesh

TO

Neha

DAUGHTER OF MR. SHANTILAL AND MRS. SHOBHANA MISTRY

SUNDAY THE FOURTEENTH OF MA...

TWO THOUSAND...

April

Budapest Spring Festival – arts festival, Budapest, Hungary

First week: Lord of the Tremors – religious thanksgiving festival, Cusco, Peru

13th–15th: Songkhran – Thai New Year

13th–15th: Pee Mai – Laos New Year

13th–15th: Chaul Chnam Thmey – Cambodian New Year

22nd: Earth Day (pp 084–085)

23rd: Feast of St. George – saint's day, Skiros, Greece; Barcelona, Spain

27: Horse Day – Turkmenistan

Virgin Islands Carnival – street festival, St. Thomas, Virgin Islands

Matsuri (pp 086–087)

FESTIVAL FACTS

EARTH DAY

- Earth Day, with its felicitous rhyme with "birthday," is a somewhat disputed annual celebration of the planet on which we live, usually held to highlight ecological concerns.

- Some groups celebrate it on the March equinox following the example set by the United Nations, but more commonly it is celebrated on April 22, sometimes as part of a week-long celebration.

- There is no standard agreed design, logo, flag, or iconography for the event, and several rival images are in circulation.

Earth Day Pledge
★ ★ ★ ★ ★ ★ ★ ★ ★ ★ ★ ★ ★ ★ ★

Design
Go Natur'l Studio

Client
Rustle the Leaf

Format
Promotional poster

Country
USA

Go Natur'l designed this poster to deliver the message behind Earth Day in a humorous way. Rustle the Leaf began life as a comic-strip character and went on to star in *Rustle the Leaf's Earth Day Book*, a 16-page educational book with comics, puzzles, and games, aimed at school students.

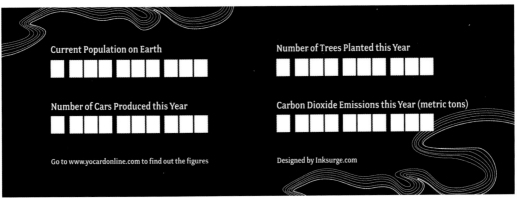

Current Population on Earth

Number of Trees Planted this Year

Number of Cars Produced this Year

Carbon Dioxide Emissions this Year (metric tons)

Go to www.yocardonline.com to find out the figures

Designed by Inksurge.com

Earth Day Stationery

Studio
Inksurge

Design
Joyce Tai

Art Direction
Rex Advincula, Joyce Tai

Client
Yocards

Format
Bookmarks/postcards

Country
The Philippines

Inksurge developed this postcard/bookmark to celebrate Earth Day. While the front has an enticing illustration with little details to pull the viewer in, the reverse carries a set of questions to be answered, designed to make people consider the ecological damage being done to the planet.

The cards were distributed through 150 outlets across the country between April 16 and April 22, the dates on which the event is celebrated in the Philippines.

Facing Page:
Nineteenth-century woodprint of a Kabuki actor standing
under cherry blossom, by Utagawa Kuniyoshi
This Page:
Below: Festive lantern hanging from the branch
of a cherry tree in blossom
Bottom: Flowers being carried in Kyoto's Aoi Matsuri parade

© naitokz/flickr

FESTIVAL FACTS

MATSURI

- In Japan, seasonal festivals or *Matsuri* are closely connected with Shinto rites and agriculture, primarily the cultivation of rice. Festivals are held in spring to encourage a good crop, and fall festivals (see p 150) are held to give thanks for a plentiful harvest.

- Viewing cherry blossom (*Sakura*) in spring is another ancient Japanese practice and is enshrined in the custom known as *Hanami*. Likewise, viewing the colors of fall, in particular the spectacular red, yellow, and orange leaves of maple trees, is formalized into the practice of *Momiji Gari*. The festival itself is known as the *Momiji Matsuri*.

- Dates for the *Matsuri* are flexible, depending on local convention, and festivals are largely staged according to when the blossoms or colors are at their peak in a particular part of the country. Expatriate communities also celebrate the festivals according to blossoms and leaves rather than particular dates.

- Both the spring and fall festivities have a rich iconography developed through centuries of poetry and image-making, through the practice of flower arranging (*Ikebana*), and the ornamentation of kimonos.

- Held on May 15, the Aoi Matsuri is an annual festival that has been celebrated in Kyoto for over 1,000 years. Now more a pageant than a festival, it perpetuates customs of the Heian era (794–1185) and takes its name from the hollyhock flowers that decorate the floats as they progress from the imperial palace to two Shinto shrines.

© Mshades/flickr

May

1st: May Day (pp 090–091)

5th: Cinco de Mayo – commemoration of victory over the French Foreign Legion, Pueblo, Mexico

8th: World Red Cross and Red Crescent Day – to celebrate and promote peace

Vesak Day (pp 092–093)

Rose Festival – Dades Valley, Morocco

Prague Spring Festival – classical music festival, Prague, Czech Republic

2nd Sunday: Mother's Day (pp 094–095)

17th: Liberation Day – Democratic People's Republic of Congo's independence day

17th: Syttende Mai/Grunnlovsdagen – Norway's independence/constitution day

Karneval der Kulturen – culture festival, Berlin, Germany

Ciclo di Spettacoli Classici – festival of Greek theater, Syracuse, Sicily, Italy

Carnival – street festival, Vilnius, Lithuania

FESTIVAL FACTS

MAY DAY

Recreation of a traditional Maypole at
Scarborough Renaissance Festival in Texas

© Marlene S/flickr

- May Day, usually celebrated on May 1, is a festival with a complicated background. For many in the northern hemisphere it is seen as the first day of summer, and various pre-Christian rites and ceremonies are preserved in its celebration. In northern and central Europe it is a time when various folkloric traditions come to the fore, particularly dancing around a Maypole and other folk-dancing traditions. It also merges with the anarchic celebration of Walpurgis Night (or the night of the witches) in Germany and Nordic countries, when pagan rituals, involving bonfires and general tomfoolery, are re-enacted.

- For many May Day is also a day of celebration of and protest for the Left and the labor movement. Also called International Workers' Day, this has its origins in nineteenth-century socialism, and is often marked with rallies in support of workers' rights around the world.

- In socialist and communist countries it is a major holiday marked with large-scale public ceremonies. In the USA and Canada, Labor Day takes place in the fall to avoid socialist connotations, but despite the lack of formal sanction, May Day parades still take place.

- For the folkloric May Day of central and northern Europe the main visual device is the flower as a symbol of fertility and summer. Girls are normally dressed in white, and there are various traditions surrounding the May Queen, a girl who is selected to lead the festivities and start the dancing. Following the dismantling of the former communist states, there is no formal iconography for the political May Day.

Colorful banners being carried by protesters
at the May Day parade in New York in 2005

FESTIVAL FACTS

VESAK DAY
(ALSO WESAK, VAISAK, OR BUDDHA DAY)

- Vesak Day is the principal festivity in the Buddhist calendar, marking, simultaneously, the Buddha's birth, enlightenment, and death (Parinirvana).

- Its spelling, form, and date vary according to the branch of Buddhism and locality, but it is most often held on the full moon in the month of May.

- It is celebrated in various ways with the common aim of providing people with the opportunity to re-engage with the principles of Buddhism.

- In many places offerings are brought to temples, where monks then lead meditation and teaching sessions.

- Vesak is a general time of joy. Homes are cleaned and various graphics, in the form of flags, posters, and paper lanterns, are used to decorate private and public spaces to express that joy. In Sri Lanka celebrations carry on for a week, during which time the consumption of alcohol and meat is prohibited.

- Various images are used for Vesak, including the image of the Buddha as a baby, but the most common is the hoisting of the Buddhist flag. This is a recent innovation intended as a nonsectarian image to unite the various schools and traditions of Buddhism. Designed in 1880 in Sri Lanka, it was adopted as the International Buddhist Flag by the 1952 Buddhist World Council. It is made up of six strips: blue (universal compassion), yellow (the Middle Path), red (blessings), white (purity and liberation), and orange (wisdom), and a final strip composed of short horizonatal blocks of these five colors.

Facing Page:

Top: Buddhist flag

Middle: Lanterns hung in Union Square, New York City, in celebration of Vesak Day

Bottom: In Japan the Buddha's birthday is known as Hana Matsuri and temples set up shrines that merge with spring flower festivities

This Page:

Ahead of Vesak Day in 2001, Malaysian-Chinese calligrapher Kenny Chen used giant brushes on huge reams of paper to write the words "Namo Amituofo," or "the Buddha of Infinite Light and Life"

FESTIVAL FACTS

MOTHER'S DAY

Homemade cards, as a sincere token of affection, rival commercial cards for this celebration

© Jose Luis Pelaez, Inc./Blend Images/Corbis

- Mother's Day is now celebrated in many places around the world. It tends to be a particularly commercialized festivity: in the USA in 2008, according to the National Retail Federation, the average consumer spent nearly $140 to mark the occasion with gifts such as flowers, meals in restaurants, cards, and jewelry.

- The establishment of the event in the USA owes much to the nineteenth-century activist Julia Ward Howe, who was horrified by its subsequent commercialism. Yet while it is quite a recent event in many countries, it does plug into many ancient rites celebrating fertility and motherhood.

- While the majority of countries celebrate Mother's Day on the second Sunday of May, other dates are also used. These range from the second Sunday in February in Norway to December 22 in Indonesia. In the UK and Ireland,where it is also known as "Mothering Sunday," Mother's Day is celebrated on the fourth Sunday in Lent.

- While there is no strict iconography, principal images include flowers (often carnations) and hearts, but any imagery or colors that are associated with femininity can be used.

Mother's Day Greetings

★ ★ ★ ★ ★ ★ ★ ★ ★ ★ ★ ★ ★ ★ ★ ★

Studio
Ellen Crimi-Trent, Inc.

Design and Illustration
Ellen Crimi-Trent

Client
Self-initiated

Format
Card

Country
USA

For Ellen Crimi-Trent birds are a natural choice and a fitting image for Mother's Day. "When I think of birds I think of the mother sitting on her eggs and feeding her chicks." Ellen plays with pattern to give each bird a different character. Even the backgrounds are given a distinctive treatment. The bright colors and and simple shapes of the birds give these cards a playful character.

June

Smart Light Festival Identity ▾

★ ★

Studio
Frost Design

Design
Quan Payne, Vince Frost,
Anthony Donovan

Client
Smart Light Festival

Format
Logo, website

Country
Australia

Smart Light Festival, an event held in Sydney's central business district in May and June 2009, sought to educate consumers and designers about the new generation of more eco-friendly lighting products and technologies. Local design group Frost developed a simple logo that plays on a modern energy-saving light bulb along with a simple website that relies on light effects.

Hove Festival Poster ▸

★ ★ ★ ★ ★ ★ ★ ★ ★ ★ ★ ★ ★ ★ ★ ★

Studio
Neighbour

Design
Samuel Muir, Phil Sims

Illustration
Ian Stevenson

Client
Hove Festival

Format
Poster

Country
Norway

While getting cold or muddy by camping on-site is a treasured feature of many festivals around the world, in Norway the first time this was allowed was in 2007 at the Hove Festival. Held outside the city of Arendal, it features international and local groups. For the poster advertising the first festival, its designers at Neighbour, in London, asked illustrator Ian Stevenson to imagine what the festival would look like at night.

Fête de la Musique Merchandise

★ ★ ★ ★ ★ ★ ★ ★ ★ ★ ★ ★ ★ ★ ★

Studio

Inksurge

Design

Rex Advincul, Joyce Tai

Client

Pulp magazine

Format

Poster, T-shirt

Country

The Philippines

Fête de la Musique, or World Music Day, is a recent festival inaugurated in France. American musician Joel Cohen first had the idea for such a festival in the mid-1970s. Musicians, either famous and established or amateur, give free concerts in the street. The festival has caught on in many countries around the world, and is usually celebrated at the time of the summer solstice. For the Philippine event in 2007, hosted by *Pulp* magazine, Inksurge created a busy, fun, and informal graphic that was used for both the promotional posters and T-shirts. Four different designs were developed to cover different genres of music: hip-hop, rock, blues, and general music.

Refugee Week Identity
★ ★ ★ ★ ★ ★ ★ ★ ★ ★ ★ ★ ★ ★ ★ ★

Studio
CHK Design

Design and Art Direction
Christian Küsters,
Hannah Dumphy

Photography
Nana Varkeropoulou

Client
Refugee Week

Format
Logo, banners, balloons,
posters, downloadable
graphics, flyers

Country
UK

Refugee Week is a UK-wide event
that has been celebrated since
1998 to dissolve tensions between
refugees and asylum seekers and
the other communities living in the
country. A variety of different events
are held across the nation with the
aim of bringing people from different
cultures together. London-based
designer Christian Küsters devised
an identity and full suite of products
for the 2006 event, and these have
been used since. The logo's many
different colored dots make the point
eloquently and subtly, and the rest of
the graphics have been kept simple
so they can be downloaded, printed,
and reproduced easily by the many
people organizing the various events
that make up the celebration.

Refugee Week

Refugee Week is a UK wide program
me of cultural and educational even
ts which celebrates the contribution
refugees make to life in the UK, and
aims to encourage encounters and b
etter understanding between comm
unities.

19 – 25 June 2006

Event

Address

Date

For more information about Refugee Week or events in your
area please visit our website: www.refugeeweek.org.uk or
telephone: +44 (0)20 7346 6752. Refugee Week Wales: +44 (0)29
2043 2990, Refugee Week Scotland: +44 (0)14 1223 7939.

Refugee
Week

Home Office

COMIC
RELIEF

FESTIVAL FACTS

GAY PRIDE

- Overturning centuries of persecution around the world, a group of gay men defied police brutality in a gay bar in New York in 1969, sparking a riot that gave rise to modern gay activism.

- Gay Pride has blossomed into an event celebrated in cities around the world, where gay men and women, bisexuals, and transgendered people celebrate their presence and community.

- Festivals and parties are staged to coincide with the carnivalesque main parade. It is held on different days around the world, allowing people to travel and join in more than one celebration. New York, its spiritual birthplace, holds the event on various dates in June.

- The "Rainbow Flag" is now the most common image of Gay Pride. Originally devised by Gilbert Baker in San Francisco in 1978, it has since been simplified into the design seen here. Made up of stripes of red, orange, yellow, green, blue, and purple, it is intended to graphically represent the richness of diversity.

Facing Page:
A giant rainbow flag being carried down Fifth Avenue in New York as part of the Gay Pride parade

Washington Ballet Annual Ball Invitations

★ ★

Studio
Design Army

Design
Julia Ames, Pum Lefebure,
Jake Lefebure

Client
The Washington Ballet

Format
Invitation

Country
USA

The Beatles/Bach Project brought together two very contrasting styles of music and choreography for a series of performances at The Washington Ballet. For its annual gala ball, the Ballet decided to adopt the theme of the show, giving Design Army a rich vein of graphics to tap into. The result was a series of five records that were in fact invitations, with all the relevant information contained on the B-side. These were slipped into vellum jackets and sent out in eye-catching fluorescent orange envelopes.

FIFA World Cup Promotion

Design
Nick Clark Design

Client
Royal Bank of Scotland

Format
Invitation, table soccer kit, passport

Country
UK

The FIFA World Cup was held in Germany in 2006, and like many other companies, the Royal Bank of Scotland used the event for their corporate hospitality. London designers Nick Clark Design devised a campaign with a selection of materials that added up to quite a plush package. The main invitation was printed on felt so that is could also serve as a "pitch" for the retro-styled table soccer set of past winners that came with it. Guides to the various cities in which the FIFA World Cup was being held, styled in the form of passports, were also sent to guests. The bespoke plastic figurines were made in China.

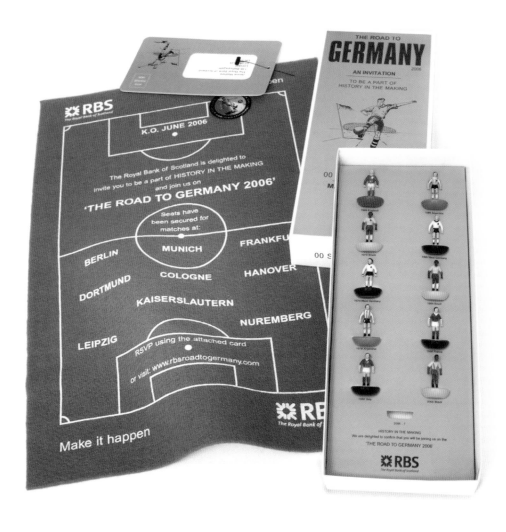

FESTIVAL FACTS

PALIO DI SIENA

Below Right: A liveried jockey in the main square—the Piazza del Campo—where the race takes place

Below: Representatives of the different *contrade* parade their respective banners and costumes

- Medieval festivals in Europe have largely become stilted, staged affairs directed at tourists. Not so the Palio, held annually in the exquisite medieval Italian city of Siena, in the heart of Tuscany.

- Medieval customs have been maintained with surprising conviction, including the division of the city into 17 ancient *contrade* or districts, with their own heraldry, liveries, and names such as *Aquila* (eagle) or *Leocorno* (unicorn). Citizens feel a fierce allegiance to their *contrade*, and rivalry with the others in the city comes to a head in the annual Palio.

- The Palio is a horse race around the shell-shaped central town square in front of the town hall. Each *contrada* fields a horse. The race is held twice a year, on June 2 and August 16, and is preceded by an extravagant medieval pageant.

- The winner of the race is presented with a painted silk banner, or *palio*, from which the event takes its name.

Birthdays & Anniversaries

Birth Announcement

★ ★

Design
Carin Goldberg

Client
Friend

Format
Card

Country
USA

When a friend gave birth to her daughter Molly, Carin Goldberg created this card to announce her arrival. It uses a montage of styles that combine to create a soft and gentle image with an element of surprise that is perfect for the event being shared and celebrated.

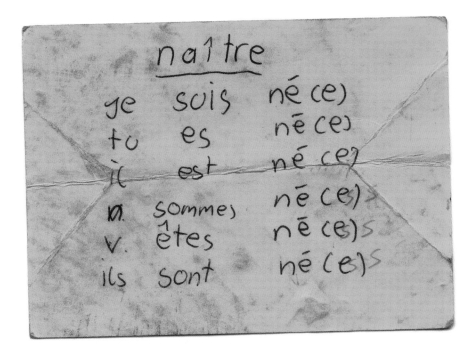

Birth Announcement

★ ★

Studio
Satellites Mistaken For Stars

Design
Alexander Egger

Client
Self-initiated

Format
Card

Country
Austria

To commemorate the birth of a
baby, Vienna-based designer/artist/
writer/musician Alexander Egger
produced this deliberately stark card.
In ballpoint pen, on a scrap of card,
he simply conjugates the verb
"to be born" in French, teasingly
withholding any further information
or specifics, such as the date of birth
and the name and sex of the child,
or who he/she was born to.

Birth Announcement

★ ★

Design
Carol García del Busto

Client
Self-initiated

Format
Card, invitation, envelope

Country
Spain

The big blue eyes of Natalia, the baby niece of Barcelona-based designer Carol García del Busto, caught the attention of everyone who met her, so when she created invitations to Natalia's baptism and the reception that followed, Carol decided to make those blue eyes the main feature. Like the baby, the invitation is tiny. It features two blue modeling eyes which move as the card is handled and removed from its quirky envelope of handmade stock with various colorful little additions. The text on the rear of the card, detailing the time and location of the celebration, is written in the first person, as though Natalia is doing the inviting herself. The edge of the card is wavy to suggest the softness of the baby's world.

beautiful eyes...

Natalia Pallás García del Busto
Hoy, 4 de febrero de 2007 es el día de mi bautizo,
a las 12.00 de la mañana en la Iglesia de San Francisco
y mis padrinos son Luis y Carol.
Mis padres Natalia y Jorge están muy contentos de celebrarlo con vosotros.

FESTIVAL FACTS

BAR MITZVAH AND BAT MITZVAH

- Under Jewish law boys become responsible for their actions at the age of 13, and girls at the age of 12. The expression bar mitzvah (bat mitzvah for girls) refers to the boy or girl being a son or daughter of the Commandments, and it is something that automatically happens on the appropriate birthday. Relatively recently this rite of passage, which often coincides with puberty, has developed into an event that is often lavishly and enthusiastically celebrated, and the term bar (or bat) mitzvah is now commonly, yet erroneously, taken to refer to the ceremony rather than the boy or girl celebrating their maturity.

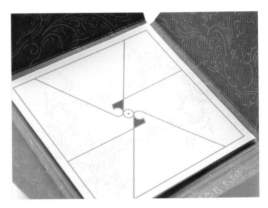

- After a religious ceremony at which the bar mitzvah reads from the Torah (Orthodox Jews do not permit the bat mitzvah to read the Torah), there is usually an elaborate reception. Much like a wedding, this is attended by friends and family who bring gifts, often in multiples of 18.

- Given Judaism's wariness of imagery leading to idolatry (from the Ten Commandments), invitations are usually abstract in nature, relying on typography and Hebrew text for their decoration.

Photography: Brion McCarthy, apparitionstudio.com

Bat Mitzvah Invitation

* *

Studio
Siquis

Design
Greg Bennett

Client
Jill Rosenstein,
Marc Rosenstein

Format
Invitation, stationery

Country
USA

To celebrate the calling of their daughter Jamie to read the Torah as a bat mitzvah, Jill and Marc Rosenstein asked designer Greg Bennett to come up with something that would not only celebrate the event in style, but would also reflect their daughter's interests and the location of the reception at the Baltimore Museum of Art. As Jamie was a keen lacrosse player, and played as number 56, these subjects were treated to an abstract typographic design that would function as the decoration and, hopefully, a talking point. A custom-made wax seal, which featured calligraphy, held the extensive invitation together. By printing on lavish Neenah Paper's EAMES Painting Collection canvas finish paper, a connection was made to the reception's location. Posters with graphics featuring photographs of Jamie also decorated the reception. As well as invitations and posters, a suite of other materials including RSVP cards, table markers, and thank-you cards was printed, directional signage was devised, and Moleskine sketchbooks adorned with the graphics of the event were given out as gifts.

ZADAR, 1807. – 2007.
200 GODINA

Pokrovitelj:
Hrvatska akademija znanosti i umjetnosti

Organizatori svečanosti:
Nacionalna i sveučilišna knjižnica u Zagrebu
Gradska knjižnica Zadar

Suorganizatori:
Grad Zadar
Sveučilište u Zadru
Općina Novigrad

Program:
Petak, 29. lipnja 2007.

ZADAR
10.00 sati Gradska loža, Svečanost obilježavanja 200. obljetnice prve hrvatske čitaonice
Predstavu Govorite li hrvatski? izvodi Joško Ševo

11.00 sati Narodni trg, Glazbeno-scenska svečanost
Scenu Pervoj od slave iz Planina Petra Zoranića izvodi Kazalište lutaka Zadar

NOVIGRAD
12.30 sati Otvaranje Knjižnice i čitaonice Novigrad
13.00 sati prigodni program

Obrazloženje:
Uz grad Zadar ove 2007. godine vezuje se iznimno značajna obljetnica za hrvatsku knjigu i osobito kulturu čitanja u Hrvata. Naime, pred dvije stotine godina, odnosno koncem lipnja godine 1807., u Zadru bilježimo važan nadnevak za hrvatsku čitaonicu točno povijest: u tom je gradu osnovana je prva hrvatska čitaonica Družba od štenja. Ovaj važan nadnevak u nekom se stoljeće povezati s onim prošlogodišnjim kada se u Zadru obilježila 200. obljetnica čitanja u novina na Kraljskog Dalmatina što je izlazio od 1806. do 1810. Ta dva vrijedna godišnji jubilej iz razdoblje u našem krajevima, uz ostalo povezati koja se nalazila čelu oba projekta, naime, upravo tu Dalmatina Bartolo Benincasa ... podnesak dalmatinske čitaonice i prvi predsjednik. On u ime grupe Kraljskog intelektualaca u travnju 1807., u ... uluku kojom odobrava vladi, već iduće mjeseca, to je 26. svibnja Vincenzo Dandolo donosi duluku ... rhu promicanja hrvatske knji ... nivanje čitaonice u Zad ... Tako je, 30. lipnja 1807., otvorena prva ja ... itutii ... tska? Jednostavno, njezina je ... janskom: Gabinetto di lettura) – i taj je važan nadnevak valjalo ... pitetom ... razna Casina, pa tako i zadarski ... će kulture u Z ... upravo tu čitaonica, nadnevak uki ... nije nigda bi ... žba od štenja i redovito je prim ... bila da bude upravo u Z ... čitaonica, a ne nešto drugo ... ila je hrvatsko na hrvatskom jeziku tada nije ... nobile, osnovan godine 1750. Dalje, čitaonica iz 1807. nosila je hrvatsko ... alo. Ta je ustanova osnovana po ... ostalu recentni period ..., i prve hrvatske novine Kraljski Dalmatin. Drugih ... Lesegesellschaft, Lekturkabine ... prema tome zadarsk ... Družba od štenja nije mogla nabavljati, Cabinet ra ... m europskim zemljama. Čita ... slična društva s ... miranje Engleskoj, zatim u Francuskoj i drugim knji ..., te posebno književna peri ... kim ... su se najprije ... vile u društva, a u njima se i navode brojne knjig ... Stipan Štefić darovao ... gradana. Medu ... nabavljati. Čitaonica je posjedovala i velik broj knjiga ... čitanja tu su sv ... nenadmašivu Diderotovu Enciklopediju. je vrijedan doprinos knjižnici hrvatski intelektualci ... od št ... mnogi korisni razgovori o raznim pitanjima U njoj su se okupljali mnogi hrvatski ... zasigurno hrvats ... važno žarište kulturnog i političkog mnijenja svekolikog narodnog života, pa je zasigurno hrvats ... e moglo dobiti na čitanje bili su, uz talijanske i ne samo grada, već cijele pokrajine. U fondu knjiga i ... u Zadru početkom XIX. st. s područja religijske kulture i francuske, i brojni hrvatski naslovi, od kojih i oni tiskani ... Čitaonica je bila smještena u sklopu kompleksa samostana sv. Krševana. knjiżevnosti, politike, prava i poljodjelstva. ... na važan jubilej kojega valja ove godine obilježiti: 200 GODINA PRVE Stoga, doista smatram važnim podsjetiti ... e, i predložiti da se taj jubilej prigodno obilježi 30. lipnja 2007., na sam dan dvjestote obljetnice, HRVATSKE ČITAONICE ... svečanostima i otvaranjem nove knjižnice i čitaonice u Novigradu, ojačiti javna svijest o potrebi čime će, prigodnim ... ČITANJA I PROMICANJA KNJIGE kao nezaobilaznoj pretpostavki ostvarenja strateškog cilja naše jačanja KULTURE ... postane "zemlja znanja". države – da Hrvatska

prva
hrvatska
čitaonica
družba
od štenja

First Birthday Invitation ▴

★ ★

Studio
Design Army

Design and Art Direction
Lee Monroe, Pum Lefebure,
Jake Lefebure

Client
Self-initiated

Format
Invitation

Country
USA

"Sophie Lefebure was turning 1, and having designer parents she needed a super-cool invite," explains Jake Lefebure, proud father and creative director of Design Army. The invitation is a set of hand-assembled, cut, and folded blocks that have the letters S, O, P, H, E, and the number 1 printed on the sides, the idea being that

Sophie would literally "turn" 1. The blocks were packaged in a custom vellum sheet that folds up to act as a carrier. "It took a lot of time to put the invite together, but thankfully she will never be 1 again," adds Lefebure.

Croatian Reading Room Bicentenary Poster ◂

★ ★

Studio
Studio International

Design
Boris Ljubicic

Client
National and University
Library, Croatia

Format
Poster

Country
Croatia

For a poster celebrating the 200th anniversary of the first Croatian reading room, located in the town of Zadar, designer Boris Ljubicic created an image that is, fittingly, all about reading. The numerals making up 200 appear, at first sight, to be a pair of old-fashioned spectacles casting

a shadow across the text, the curved lines of which suggest an open book. It is an image that is witty and cerebral. The seemingly abstract text is actually intended to be read—it contains all the relevant information about the library and the celebration of its anniversary.

Joint 70th/80th Birthday Party Invitation

★ ★

Studio
Playful

Design
Pablo Alfieri

Client
Self-initiated

Format
Flyer

Country
Argentina

In June 2008 designer Pablo Alfieri's mother and stepfather were having a lunch to celebrate their 70th and 80th birthdays, respectively. To mark the occasion, which took place in a traditional Argentinean restaurant,

Alfieri designed a flyer that would act as an invitation to the event. Taking the two significant numbers, he concentrated on creating a beautiful design that would give a distinctly festive and upbeat feel.

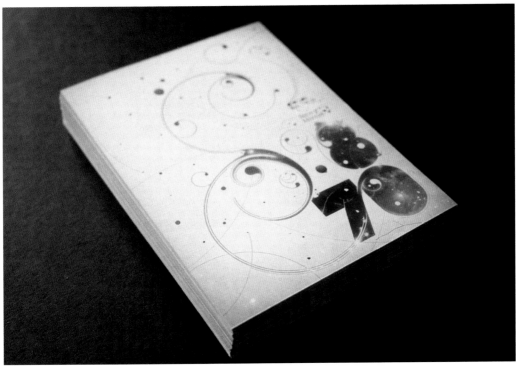

Helvetica 50th Anniversary Poster

★ ★

Studio
Studio International

Design
Boris Ljubicic

Client
Linotype

Format
Poster

Country
Croatia/Switzerland

In 2007 Linotype celebrated the passing of 50 years since the launch of Helvetica, the typeface that brought Swiss modernism into millions of people's lives. The foundry organized a poster competition to mark the event. Croatian designer Boris Ljubicic's entry made reference to another icon of Switzerland—the army knife—with font samples taking the place of blades. Set along the bottom is the motto, "Helvetica is not typography, it's lettering." Ljubicic explains that this "is meant to show that Helvetica has outgrown itself and become far more than typography, just as the Swiss knife has become so much more than a knife. It can do anything."

Nobel Prize Centenary Stamps

★ ★

Studio
HGV

Design
Pierre Vermeir

Client
Royal Mail

Format
Postage stamps

Country
UK

Ever since the generous bequest of the Swedish polymath Alfred Nobel and the inauguration of the Nobel Prize in 1901, the award has been closely watched internationally and few awards can match it for prestige. Initially five awards were issued, celebrating the finest minds or most important contributions in physics, chemistry, physiology or medicine, literature, and peace. In the 1960s an award for economics was added. To celebrate 100 years of the event, the Royal Mail in the UK commissioned HGV to create a set of stamps commemorating each of the prizes. Pierre Vermeir of HGV developed an appropriate design for each. So, for instance, for chemistry, the stamp was printed with thermo-chromatic ink that displayed an ion in a molecule when touched; for economics it was printed with the same gravure techniques as those used for bank-notes; and for literature, the stamp features an entire poem by T. S. Eliot that can actually be read with the aid of a magnifying glass.

80th Birthday T-shirt

★ ★

Studio

Topos Graphics

Design

Seth Labenz, Roy Rub

Client

Regina Bradley Luchtel

Format

T-shirt

Country

USA

Topos Graphics were commissioned to design a T-shirt to commemorate the celebration of Jean Luchtel's 80th birthday. The logo it created is a stylization of the numerals 8 and 0, and in place of the manufacturer's tag are the following lines: "Regina Bradley Luchtel was born on August 13, 1928 in Shickley, NE and will celebrate 80 years this year, 2008. Cheers to a continued line of life to be cherished and admired on her birthday, celebrated with family and friends in Pine Top, AZ."

1928

2008

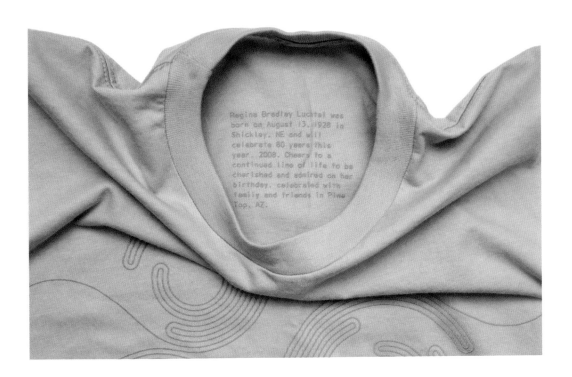

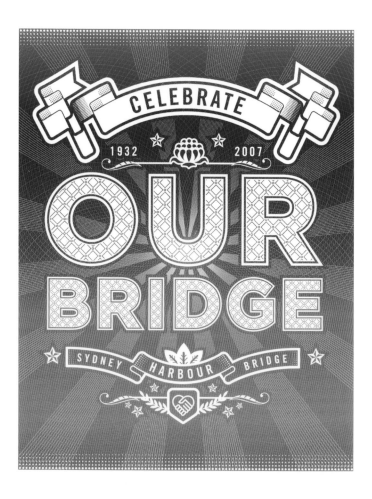

Sydney Harbour Bridge 75th Anniversary Campaign

★ ★

Design
Deuce Design

Client
New South Wales
Premier's Department

Format
Identity, posters, banners,
caps, flags, marketing
materials

Country
Australia

Along with the nearby Sydney Opera House, the Sydney Harbour Bridge is one of the most readily identifiable icons of Australia. In March 2007, the steel structure celebrated its 75th anniversary, something the city wanted to mark in style. Roads were closed and various events arranged, including an Aboriginal smoking ceremony. Deuce Design was entrusted with the extensive graphics for the occasion, including bright gold-and-green souvenir caps that were distributed to the pedestrian visitors and participants.

"The brief was to attract the widest possible demographic, from toddlers to octogenarians, via loud, bright, exciting, and fun graphics," recounts Deuce director Sophie Tatlow. "Central to the identity was the fluoro-pop psychedelic twist on recognized Australian icons, featuring native animals, local flora and fauna, surfboards, boats, Holden cars, kitsch Australiana, and two hands holding the bridge."

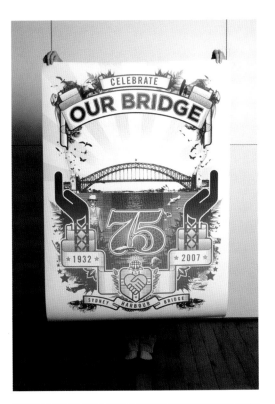

July

4th: Independence Day (p 128)

V&A Village Fête (p 129)

14th: Bastille Day (pp 132–133)

Caribana – street festival, Toronto, Canada

Balinese Prayer Offerings (p 131)

Roskilde Music Festival – Roskilde, Denmark

Rouen Armada – street festival, Rouen, France

Taormina Arte – arts festival, Taormina, Sicily, Italy

St. Christopher Summer Festival – jazz festival, Vilnius, Lithuania

Summer Party (p 130)

T in the Park – music festival, Kinross, Scotland

Montreux Jazz Festival – Montreux, Switzerland

Forma Nova (pp 134–135)

Te Maeva Nui Festival – the Cook Islands' independence celebrations

Independence Day (USA) E-greetings

★ ★ ★ ★ ★ ★ ★ ★ ★ ★ ★ ★ ★ ★ ★

Studio
Kame Design

Design
Joachim Müller-Lancé

Client
Self-initiated

Format
E-card

Country
USA

On July 4, 1776, the USA declared independence from its then colonial master Great Britain. This founding act has always been the country's principal secular celebration, marked with much pomp and many patriotic festivities ranging from fireworks displays to barbecues. Whatever the format, the iconography for the event always involves elements drawn from the stars and stripes of the US flag, and its three colors: red, white, and blue. These two interpretations are e-greetings by a German designer based in San Francisco. For the 2007 design he used "a pompous overblown Xanadu disco-style as an ironic nod to Californian campness," while for the following year some of the typical features of Independence Day celebrations are gate-crashed by sausages—a humorous nod to his own nationality.

4ᵀᴴ OF JULY 2008

V&A Village Fête Installation

★ ★ ★ ★ ★ ★ ★ ★ ★ ★ ★ ★ ★ ★ ★

Design
Multistorey

Carpentry
Simon Casey

Client
Scarlet Projects (curators of the event)

Format
Poster, model

Country
UK

Rodeo, and the distinctive typography of the Wild West, are not things you immediately associate with the genteel surroundings of London's Kensington, or the British tradition of the village fête. Traditionally the fête (for arcane reasons it is British custom to use the French for "party") is a frumpy, homespun affair. But the event was reinterpreted for the courtyard of the Victoria & Albert Museum, and rather than moms selling homemade cakes and preserves, various designers and craftspeople touted their wares. Among them was graphic design group Multistorey which produced this rodeo stall. A poster and life-sized bull were made of plywood, and people who managed to lasso the animal successfully were given a small cardboard version of it.

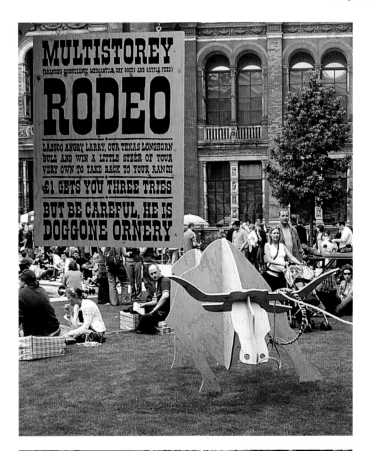

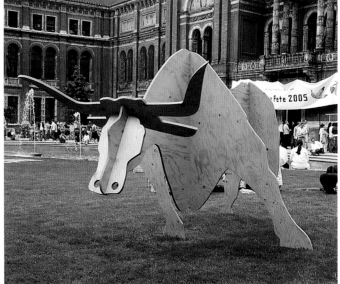

Summer Party Invitation

* *

Studio

TFI Envision Inc.

Design and Art Direction

Elizabeth P. Ball,
Mary Ellen Butkus

Client

Self-initiated

Format

Invitation

Country

USA

Like many businesses TFI Envision, a design group in Connecticut, holds a summer party to entertain friends, clients, and suppliers. In 2007 the event celebrated TFI Envision's new patio, and the informality of the event was captured with a lighthearted self-promotional campaign based around the line "be there or be square." The invitations, including "tickets" were sent out as "flat-packed cubes" for the recipients to fold into their final form.

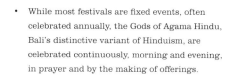

FESTIVAL FACTS

BALINESE PRAYER OFFERINGS

- While most festivals are fixed events, often celebrated annually, the Gods of Agama Hindu, Bali's distinctive variant of Hinduism, are celebrated continuously, morning and evening, in prayer and by the making of offerings.

- These offerings, or *canang sari*, take the form of a small tray made from a palm leaf, filled with all kinds of things—flowers, rice, sweets, and fruits—and finished with a stick of burning incense. Sometimes a small amount of money is also placed on the tray. The offerings themselves are placed in all manner of places: outside temples, on taxi dashboards and motorcycle panniers, and in store fronts.

- The aesthetics of Balinese prayer offerings are intrinsic to the ritual, and their preparation is seen as an art form. In Balinese Hinduism, artistic self-expression and religious observance are one, not only in the creation of these offerings, but also in the elaborately staged rituals.

- Every element of the painstakingly created offering has some symbolic significance. The main offering is associated with Shiva, the incense represents Brahma, and the holy water Vishnu.

Various offerings photographed by Tim Vinyer during a reportage visit to Bali

FESTIVAL FACTS

BASTILLE DAY

- The storming of the Bastille prison on July 14, 1789, marked the start of the French Revolution and the birth of the French Republic. The commemoration of this event is France's most important national holiday.

- The main festivities are held on the Champs-Élysées in Paris, but smaller versions take place all over the country, and in other nations as well.

- Visually, the event is dominated by the *drapeau tricolore*, with its three vertical bands of blue, white, and red symbolizing liberty, equality, and fraternity. The flag was used during the Revolution and subsequently adopted as the national flag and emblem of France.

The Red Arrows flying over the Louvre in Paris, leaving vapor trails in the colors of the French flag

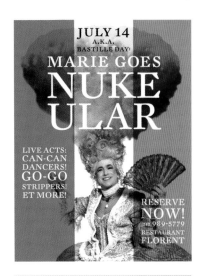

Bastille Day Promotion

* *

Design
Memo Productions, Inc.

Client
Restaurant Florent,
New York City

Format
Posters, postcards

Country
USA

France's national celebration, because of its world significance, is also celebrated abroad. The historical figures of the French Revolution are ingrained in most people's imagination, so a French restaurant in New York City's Meatpacking district was able to have some fun with the imagery as it joined in the celebrations of Bastille Day (which coincided with the owner's 50th birthday that year). Marie-Antoinette, the Queen of France who was famously guillotined during the French Revolution, is represented here as a drag queen.

Forma Nova Festival Promotion

★ ★

Studio
M&E

Design
Matthew Bolger,
Emelie Lidström

Client
Forma Nova Festival

Format
Catalog, flyers,
T-shirts, stickers

Country
Denmark/Sweden

In July 2007, the fifth Forma Nova Festival took place in Fredericia, Denmark. "It's an alternative music festival featuring mainly experimental electronic artists," explain the designers Matthew Bolger and Emelie Lidström, who are based in neighboring Sweden. "We took Forma Nova to mean 'new forms' and wanted to express this in the design. The idea was to show that this was a summer festival with a darker, more experimental twist. We wanted it to look as though someone was picking up 'new forms,' or strange berries, each in the shape of the letters spelling out the name of the festival. The person is playing with them as you would with berries in the summertime: picking and shoving them onto your fingers. The five fingers of the hand also symbolize the fifth anniversary of the festival." This striking motif was used for all the materials required for the festival, from flyers and a catalog to posters, stickers, and T-shirts.

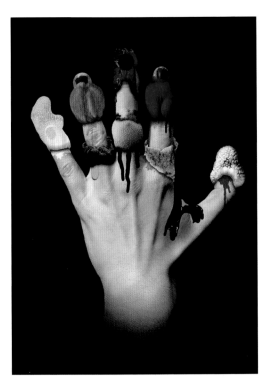

August

CCD 07 (pp 138–139)

Gay Pride Festival – Amsterdam, the Netherlands

14th: I Candelieri – thanksgiving for deliverance from plague, Sassari, Sardinia, Italy

Taormina Arte – arts festival, Taormina, Sicily, Italy

Asilah Arts Festival (p 141)

Edinburgh Festival – arts festival, Edinburgh, Scotland

Frizon (pp 142–143)

La Tomatina – street festival, Buñol, Spain

The Big Chill (pp 144–145)

Last weekend: Notting Hill Carnival (pp 140–141)

Shotan (pp 146–147)

CCD 07 Magazine

★ ★

Studio
Brighten the Corners
Design and Art Direction
Billy Kiosoglou,
Frank Philippin
Photography
Marcus Tate, Tim Mitchell
Client
Accenture Ireland
Format
Magazine
Country
Ireland/UK

Every year business consultancy Accenture Ireland stages a one-day festivity for its staff. Known as CCD or Community Communications Day, the idea is to provide an occasion at which people across the company can mingle in a creative way. In 2007 this revolved around the Accenture Fête; in essence, a series of creative events staged by employees. Brighten the Corners was commissioned to develop accompanying graphics. It created a lively news magazine, printed in full color, on newsprint, in the medium-sized Berliner format. The images document the activities of the company and also showcase a montage of personal information, such as the secrets, wishes, and dreams of the employees.

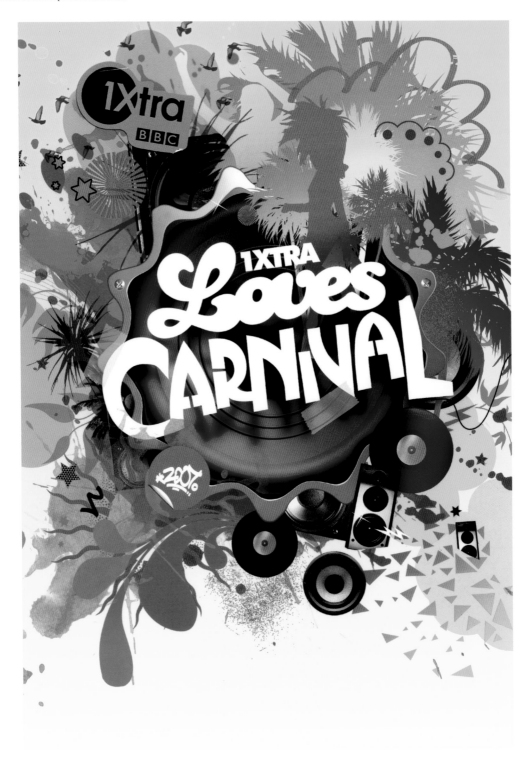

© Floris Leeuwenberg/Corbis

Notting Hill Carnival Identity ◂

★ ★ ★ ★ ★ ★ ★ ★ ★ ★ ★ ★ ★ ★

Studio
Studio Output

Design
Steve Payne

Client
BBC Radio 1XTRA

Format
Various, including flyers and floats

Country
UK

The Notting Hill Carnival is celebrated in the British late summer, at the end of August. It was first held in the 1960s by the local Trinidadian community in a part of West London that has since become very plush, but continues to be the locale for a massive street party and celebration of the Caribbean roots of many people in the UK. The Carnival is now one of the biggest outdoor festivals in Europe, with an attendance of well over 2 million people. Steel bands and costumed dancers vie with many very loud outdoor sound systems and street parties. To coincide with the event, radio station BBC 1XTRA commissioned "bright, over the top, fun" graphics from Studio Output to make people aware of the full spectrum of music it plays. The graphics were used for advertising, merchandising, flyers, and of course a float that formed part of the parade that is an intrinsic element of the festival.

FESTIVAL FACTS

ASILAH ARTS FESTIVAL

- Since 1978, the Moroccan town of Asilah has staged an international cultural festival in August. Not far from Tangiers on the northwest Atlantic coast, Asilah is characterized by distinctive, whitewashed houses and walls. During the festival, which includes music and poetry, the white walls of the town are transformed as artists are given free rein to paint temporary murals.

Top: Woman and child walking past a mural painted on the whitewashed walls of Asilah

Bottom: Mural painted by Mexican artist Eunice Vidales

© Pedro Lozano/flickr

Frizon Posters

★ ★

Design
Lobby Design

Client
EFK-UNG/Frizon Festivalen

Format
Flyers, posters

Country
Sweden

Frizon is an annual music festival held in the city of Örebro, in central Sweden. Aimed primarily at teenagers, it adopts a different theme every year. Lobby Design, based in the Swedish capital Stockholm, created the graphics for the festival in 2006 when the theme was "the road," and again the following year when it was "truth." For 2008, the surprising theme was "death," which allowed a confluence of classic rock imagery and older Christian iconography linked to the Last Judgment.

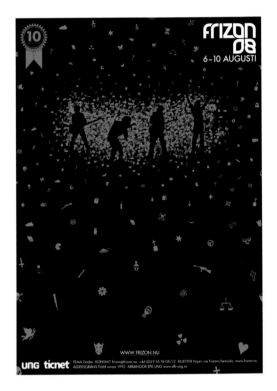

The Big Chill Promotion

★ ★

Studio
Neighbour

Design and Art Direction
Samuel Muir, Phil Sims

Client
The Big Chill

Format
Posters

Country
UK

The Big Chill is an eclectic and easy-going music festival held in a rural location in England. To advertise the festival in 2008, London designers Neighbour created these strange, yet enticing images with the photographic trick of using a "tilt-shift" lens. This has the effect of creating a surreal image with excessive blurring, making everything seem as if it were a miniature model rather than the real thing.

FESTIVAL FACTS

**SHOTAN
OR YOGURT
FESTIVAL**

- Despite being under threat, Tibetan culture continues to have some of the most sumptuous and detailed imagery imaginable. The annual Shotan (also Shoton) Festival is no exception. Taking place on the thirtieth day of the sixth Tibetan month (which usually equates to late August in the Gregorian calendar), it is a time when yogurt is eaten, yaks are raced, and Tibetan opera is watched.

- As part of the lead-up to the festival, a giant image of the Buddha is taken out of the Drepung Monastery and unfurled in front of the crowds who respond by throwing lengths of white silk known as *hada*. Bugles are blown and incense is burned. After being shown for two hours, the giant *tangka* is rolled up and put away for another year.

- *Tangkas* (or *thangkas*) are complex images designed to assist teaching and meditation in Tibetan Buddhism, and are often rolled up. The imagery allows the viewer to remember certain stories from the life of the Buddha and other deities more easily, and beyond that, it encourages a process of visualization so that the viewer can be brought into the state of the object being viewed. The highly intricate imagery follows set traditional themes and requires very detailed and sophisticated deciphering.

The annual opening of the giant *tangka* of the Buddha outside Drepung Monastery in Tibet—part of the lead-up to the Shotan Festival

September

Floriade – spring festival of flowers, Canberra, Australia

Ganesh Festival – celebration of Ganesh's birthday, Pune, Maharashtra, India

Fall Matsuri (p 150)

Treasure Island Music Festival (p 151)

Festes de la Merce – saint's day, Barcelona, Spain

Village Green Festival (pp 152–153)

21st: International Day of Peace

Ramadan (pp 154–160)

Eid el-Fitr (pp 160–161)

Last Week: Hermanus Whale Festival – South Africa

Fall Matsuri
Poster

★ ★ ★ ★ ★ ★ ★ ★ ★ ★ ★ ★ ★ ★ ★

Design
Ian Lynam Design

Client
City of Naruse
Citizen's Council

Format
Poster

Country
Japan

The Japanese divide the year into five seasons: spring, rainy season, summer, fall, and winter. *Setsubun* festivals or *matsuri* are held to celebrate the coming of each of the seaons, particularly spring and fall which, for aesthetic as well as religious and agricultural reasons, are held to be the most auspicious. The dates vary from area to area, and often depend on nature. This poster, created for the fall festival staged by the Citizen's Council of Naruse, a Tokyo neighborhood, presents simple images traditionally associated with fall and *matsuri*, and presents the date and place of the festival in a clear and simple way.

Treasure Island Music Festival Promotion

★ ★

Studio
The Small Stakes

Design
Jason Munn

Client
Treasure Island Music Festival

Format
Poster

Country
USA

Treasure Island is a man-made island lying between San Francisco and Oakland in California. Since September 2006 it has been the venue for a vibrant two-day music festival. For the second festival, held in 2007, Jason Munn of The Small Stakes, in Oakland, was commissioned to design a poster to publicize the event. He settled on an image of an overturned galleon, the bottom of which becomes a small island. The image proved very popular and was adopted as the festival's emblem.

VILL
AGE
GRE
EN.

Village Green Festival Promotion

★ ★

Studio
Thompson Brand Partners

Design and Illustration
Josh Millar

Client
Metal Culture

Format
T-shirts, flyers, posters,
badges, maps, bags,
ID cards, microsite

Country
UK

Festivals held on village greens are
an ancient tradition in England. For
a festival of arts and sport held in
Southend-on-Sea to celebrate the
launch of the cultural Olympiad, this
traditional event was given a modern
twist. Bunting, a typical feature, was
the principal inspiration for the designs
created by Thompson Brand Partners.
Called the Village Green Festival, the

organizers and designers wanted to
ensure it was green in both senses
of the word. "We wanted the job to
be 100 percent recycled. The print
was screenprinted on 100 percent
recycled card and boards," explains
designer Josh Millar. "The crew for
the festival brought in their own
T-shirts and we reused them by
screenprinting over the old graphics,

★ ★

with the Village Green logo on the front and a '100 percent recycled crew' on the back." In addition, graphics were developed for flyers, posters, badges, maps, bags, ID cards, and a microsite.

© Manjunath Kiran/epa/Corbi

FESTIVAL FACTS

RAMADAN

- A month-long event, Ramadan is the most prominent religious date in the Muslim calendar. It takes place in the ninth month of that calendar, when the Koran was revealed to the Prophet Mohammed.

- The start is often taken from the sighting of the new moon in Saudi Arabia, but there are regional divergences. As it follows a lunar calendar, it is an event that shifts considerably in the Gregorian calendar.

- Ramadan is principally a month of fasting, and requires that Muslims rise before dawn to eat the *Suhoor* meal and perform prayers; after each fourth day of prayer, they eat the *Maghrib* (sunset) meal. Night-long prayers are also encouraged.

- Ramadan is a time for contemplation, self-reformation, and spiritual cleansing. Alongside prayer, Muslims are encouraged to do good deeds.

- Ramadan comes to an end with a final fast-breaking meal, *Iftar*, which is often a lavish event lasting long into the night. The festival of the breaking of the fast is known as *Eid el-Fitr*.

The henna-painted hands of a girl in Bangalore, India, praying during the celebration of Eid el-Fitr

iCity Ramadan Promotion

★ ★

Design
Paragon Marketing
Communications

Client
iCity Kuwait

Format
Print advertisement

Country
Kuwait

In Arab countries it is not unusual for advertising to acknowledge religious events, in particular Ramadan. For iCity, an authorized Apple distributor in Kuwait, Paragon Marketing Communications created this understated ad, which takes the trademark white headphone wires of the iPod and iPhone and uses them to create the crescent moon that is the most widely recognized symbol for both Ramadan and Islam generally. Verses in elaborate calligraphy don't seem out of place in this unlikely, but successful marriage of traditional Islamic culture and American consumerism.

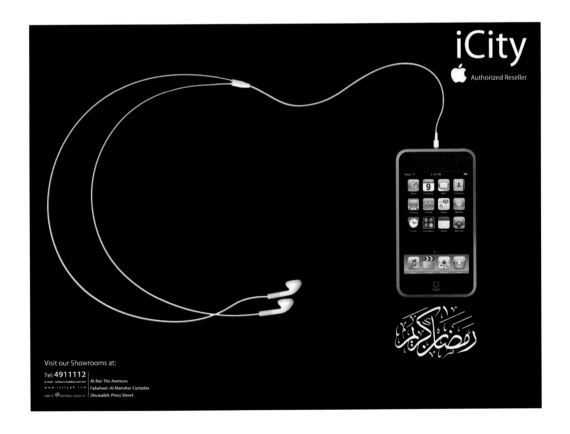

Ramadan Digital Stationery

★ ★

Design
Mohamed Eissa

Client
Self-initiated

Format
Desktop wallpaper

Country
Egypt

Geometric shapes and patterns have a religious significance in Islam. Not only does this abstraction adhere to the tradition of not representing living beings in sacred art, it also presents an image of harmony and order. These Islamic geometric and calligraphic traditions were reinterpreted digitally in a series of wallpapers for the month of Ramadan by Egyptian designer Mohamed Eissa. They are executed in different colorways to allow users to choose the one that most appeals to them.

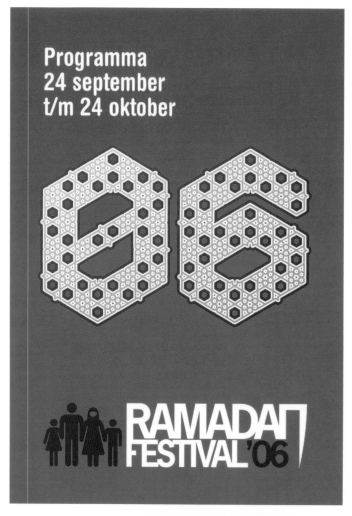

Programma
24 september
t/m 24 oktober

RAMADAN
FESTIVAL '06

Ramadan Festival Identity ◆▸

★ ★ ★ ★ ★ ★ ★ ★ ★ ★ ★ ★ ★ ★ ★ ★

Design
Because

Client
Mex-it

Format
Logo, posters

Country
The Netherlands

Since its inception in 2005, the Ramadan Festival has grown as a social and cultural event to bring together Muslims and non-Muslims. While it takes its name from the holy month of Ramadan, it consists of a variety of events to facilitate dialogue and debate. The festival was the brainchild of Amsterdam-based consultancy Mex-it, which continues to support the event. The logo for the festival and its various communications was designed by Because, part of Koeweiden Postma, a design group dedicated to working with the charitable and social sector. The event has grown in stature and has been taken up in other cities in the Netherlands and other countries, including the UK and Norway. One of the features is the invitation of Muslims to non-Muslims to an *Iftar* dinner, and the poster suggest the various dishes that might be on offer.

Komen jullie weer
bij ons eten?

RAMADAN
FESTIVAL '06

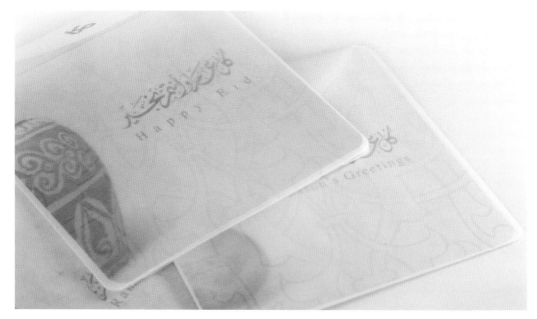

Ramadan and Eid el-Fitr Greetings

★ ★

Studio

Paragon Marketing
Communications

Design and Art Direction

Huzaifa Kakumama,
Louai Alasfahani

Client

Kuwait Projects Co. (KIPCO)

Format

Cards

Country

Kuwait

This suite of cards for the holy month of Ramadan and the feast of Eid el-Fitr at its close are designed to provide variety so that, when sent out to companies, not everyone receives the same card.

Photography of ancient pottery with geometric designs provides the main imagery alongside ornate calligraphic script. Each card has a transparent envelope shot through with a subtle geometric decoration.

Eid el-Fitr Digital Stationery

★ ★

Design
Mohamed Eissa

Client
Self-initiated

Format
Desktop wallpaper

Country
Egypt

Eid el-Fitr, the celebration that marks the end of Ramadan for Muslims, is an occasion of joy and hospitality. These two aspects were taken and interpreted graphically by young Egyptian designer Mohamed Eissa: by creating a wallpaper that could be downloaded free, it was an act of generosity, while its treatment of traditional Islamic motifs in Photoshop is exuberant. Two different versions allowed people to choose how they wished to mark the occasion on their computers. The text wishes people a "Happy Feast."

October

Women's History Month (p 164)

1st: Independence Day - Nigeria's independence day

2nd: Mahatma Gandhi's Birthday - India

Oktoberfest (p 165)

Fiesta de Santa Teresa - saint's day, Ávila, Spain

El Señor de Los Milagros - street festival, Peru

24th: United Nations Day

31st: Halloween (pp 166–171)

Women's History Month Posters

★ ★ ★ ★ ★ ★ ★ ★ ★ ★ ★ ★ ★ ★ ★ ★

Studio
Kolegram

Design and Art Direction
Martin Poirier,
Jean-Luc Denat

Client
Status of Women Canada

Format
Poster

Country
Canada

In Canada, women's rights are promoted and investigated by a dedicated government body called the Status of Women Canada, which is represented by a minister of state. Among its various activities it promotes Women's History Month in October (unlike its neighbor, the USA, which celebrates the event in March). For 2008, design group Kolegram came up with a design for the theme "Women in the lead" by presenting a series of colored bars, as if on a graph, on top of which is the international symbol of women (a circle on top of the positive sign). The 2007 event was dedicated to looking at the situation of immigrant women, and the bilingual poster made a subtle connection between the national emblem of maple leaves in fall and the different bracelets on the sleeve of the woman reaching up to touch them.

Two young women dressed in traditional dirndles present the official beer mug for the 2007 Oktoberfest

FESTIVAL FACTS

OKTOBERFEST

- In October 1810, Prince Ludwig of Bavaria got married, an event that was celebrated in characteristic Bavarian style with lots of beer being drunk. It's an event that has been repeated every year since, spiraling into the 16 days of revelry that now attracts beer drinkers from around the world.

- As the festival grew, its start date was brought forward, and it now begins in September and finishes in October. Held in enormous boisterous tents, it is a celebration of traditional Bavarian culture, costume, and food.

- The evocative, often pseudo-heraldic branding of the various breweries involved features on various items, from beer mats and T-shirts to special editions of the steins, or 1-liter beer mugs, either made of glass or ceramic. Each year a new identity is developed and used for posters and souvenirs.

Below: Halloween montage featuring zombies and ghosts from the PLAYMOBIL line of children's toys

Bottom: A particularly carefully carved Jack O'Lantern

© Anna Duncan Art/flickr

© fabbio/flickr

FESTIVAL FACTS

HALLOWEEN

- Halloween has become a major event for children in Anglo-Saxon countries despite, or perhaps because of, its macabre traditions and paraphernalia. The festivity has its origins in All Saints' Day (the word "Halloween" is a corruption or shortening of "All Hallows' Evening"), a day of commemoration of the dead in Christian culture, and it is celebrated on October 31, which is the day before All Saints' Day. But it also draws on various pagan and Celtic celebrations, such as Samhain (a Celtic festival to mark the end of the summer harvest). Both origins, in their different ways, are an engagement with the deceased and ghosts, however, it is now celebrated as a fun and lighthearted event.

- The carved pumpkin, or Jack O'Lantern, is the most common Halloween image. Pumpkins are hollowed and have spooky features cut into them, and are often illuminated by placing a lighted candle inside. The image of the illuminated Jack O'Lantern lends the festivity its characteristic colors of black and orange.

- The celebration of Halloween has become associated with the imagery of horror movies, including skeletons and vampires, and also imagery relating to the paranormal and witchcraft.

- It is common to hold bonfires, and the North American tradition of trick or treating, with children in costume walking from house to house and asking for treats is becoming more popular in other countries. Candied apples are a traditional example of these treats.

Halloween Cards

★ ★ ★ ★ ★ ★ ★ ★ ★ ★ ★ ★ ★ ★ ★

Studio
Ellen Crimi-Trent, Inc.

Design and Illustration
Ellen Crimi-Trent

Client
Self-initiated

Format
Cards

Country
USA

The typical Halloween colors are brought to life here through placing the flat-black bats against a highly textured orange background which has the effect of making it look as though the bats are flying through a storm. The ghosts, another classic Halloween image, are also given a fun treatment. Each has a strong, cartoon-like character and expression.

Halloween Greetings

★ ★ ★ ★ ★ ★ ★ ★ ★ ★ ★ ★ ★ ★ ★

Design
Marian Bantjes

Client
Self-initiated

Format
Cards

Country
Canada

Canadian illustrator Marian Bantjes sends out Halloween (and Valentine's) cards from her studio. Her favorite remains her intricate and personal design created for the greeting in 2005. Her design for the following year is appropriately eerie and contains some surprises in its delicately hand-drawn lines. "It has more than meets the eye—note the evil clown in the abdomen. And the hairs on the legs all spell the names of various phobias," says Bantjes.

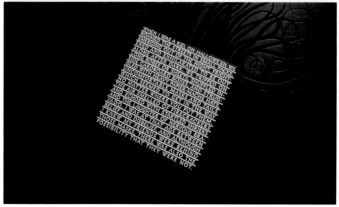

WHEN I WAS A KID, ON HALLOWE'EN WE
ROAMED THE STREETS IN SMALL PACKS,
EMERGING OUT OF THE NIGHT, FRIGHT-
ENED AND EXHILARATED TO BE OUT
ALONE AFTER DARK. WE TRIPPED ON
LONG ROBES OR SHEETS, SHUFFLED IN-
SIDE CARDBOARD BOXES, AND STRUG-
GLED WITH HEAVY PAPIER-MACHE HATS,
UNCOMFORTABLE MASKS AND TAILS
WHICH SEEMED TO GET IN THE WAY
NO MATTER WHERE YOU PUT THEM.
THE AIR SMELLED OF FIRECRACKERS
AND ECHOED WITH STARTLED SHRIEKS
AND THE LAUGHTER OF NERVOUS BRA-
VADO. I WAS AT THAT AGE BETWEEN
BELIEF AND DISBELIEF, AND ALTHOUGH
I KNEW MY FRIENDS WERE BEHIND
THOSE MASKS, THERE WAS ALSO THE
POSSIBILITY THAT THEY WERE NOT.

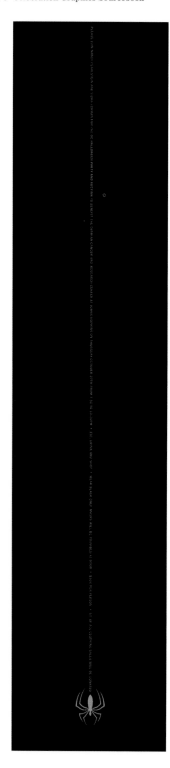

Halloween Stationery

★ ★

Studio
Design Army

Design and Art Direction
Tim Madle, Pum Lefebure, Jake Lefebure

Client
Relish

Format
Invitation

Country
USA

Relish, a Washington DC clothing store, hit upon the idea of having a Halloween party that, as well as being fun, would raise money for a good cause—research into ovarian cancer. Local graphic design group Design Army agreed to design the invitation. "The project was done pro bono so it had to be well thought out; the simple long folds and two colors (black and sliver) make for a striking invite, and the simple spider graphic dropping down from a thread of text—the invitation details—was all that we needed to make it special," explains Design Army creative director Jake Lefebure.

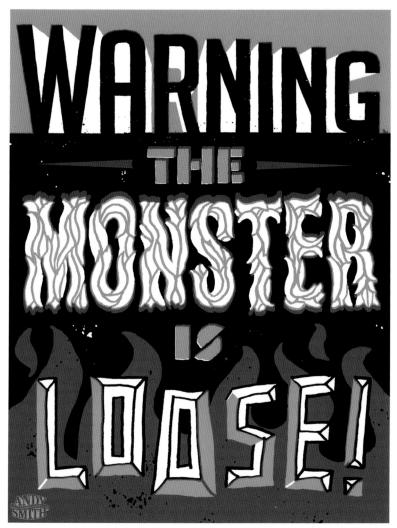

Halloween Stationery

★ ★

Design
Andy Smith

Client
Self-initiated

Format
Poster, envelope

Country
UK

For this humorous self-promotional mailer to his clients, British illustrator Andy Smith used the occasion of Halloween to make a mock-scary impression on his clients, much like children knocking at the door. Keeping to the black and orange/yellow colors traditional to the event, and including

a Jack O'Lantern or carved pumpkin on the envelope, he "warns" in his characteristic, screenprinted, hand-drawn typography that "the monster is loose."

November

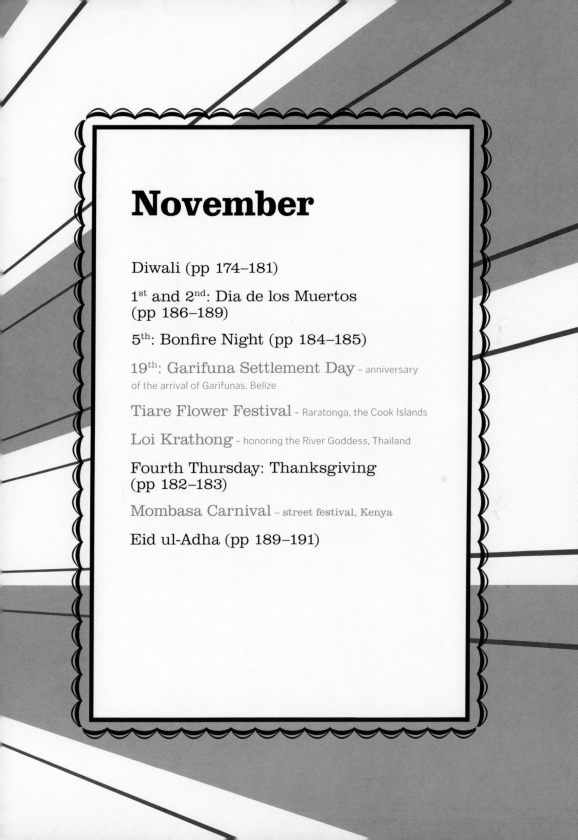

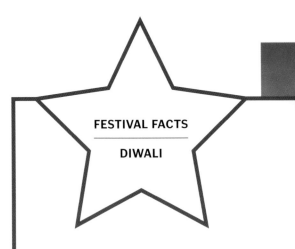

FESTIVAL FACTS

DIWALI

This Page:
Top: Diwali being celebrated at home
Bottom: The festival is known as Deepavali in Singapore. These colorful decorations are displayed in Singapore's Little India district
Facing Page:
Close-up of a modern *rangoli* or sand painting

© Subharnab Majumdar 2008/flickr

- Diwali (also spelt Divali, Dewali, Deepavali) is the main festival of Hindus. Also known as the Festival of Lights, it represents the triumph of light over darkness. This is symbolized by the burning of candles, which are the festival's main emblem.

- As well as more modern items such as cards, a variety of traditional graphics are used to celebrate Diwali, including henna designs on skin and *rangoli* (traditional Indian sand painting). Colorful star-shaped paper lanterns (*kandils*) are traditionally hung in homes to celebrate Diwali.

- *Diyas*, traditional clay lights filled with vegetable oil and a cotton wick, are preferred to more modern wax candles.

- Diwali is a five-day festival, falling during October or November, but its exact date can vary regionally within India (starting earlier in the South), and depends on the waning of the moon in the month of Ashvina.

- It is also celebrated by Sikhs, Buddhists, and Jains in the Indian subcontinent, and by people of Indian descent around the world.

Photo by Bernard Oh

Diwali Greetings

★ ★ ★ ★ ★ ★ ★ ★ ★ ★ ★ ★ ★ ★ ★

Studio
Creative ID

Design
Vaishali Shah

Photography
David West

Client
Various

Format
Cards

Country
UK/India

"During Diwali, homes are beautifully illuminated with small oil lamps or candles. This festival celebrates the victory of light over darkness," explains Vaishali Shah of UK-based design group Creative ID. "The colors we used for our card designs are therefore vibrant and rich. Our aim was to give a modern interpretation to the traditional festival of Diwali. We have used a large palette of colors and not just the traditional ones. Along with the traditional diya and flame-based designs, we have used contemporary aums [sacred symbol for the word "Om"], lotus flowers, and *rangoli* [sand painting] patterns." The choice of gold card not only gave the cards added luminescence, the color is also held to be auspicious. Some were hand-finished with small gold reflective embellishments to make them feel even more luxurious. The cards were aimed at the UK's substantial community of people with connections to the Indian subcontinent, but nonetheless carried a very brief description of the festival on their backs.

Diwali Greetings

★ ★

Design
Creative ID

Client
Self-initiated

Format
Cards

Country
UK

Benares is a Michelin-starred restaurant in London owned by chef Atul Kochhar. For Diwali in 2008, the restaurant asked Creative ID to develop cards to celebrate the Festival of Lights. The cards were handmade with gold card and vibrant sari fabrics, and some also featured the actual spices used in Indian cooking. A recipe was included, and the cards were a limited edition, each numbered and signed by Kochhar.

Diwali Greetings

★ ★

Design
Neha Motipara

Client
Self-initiated

Format
Card

Country
USA

Feeling there were no modern, well-designed greeting cards for Diwali available in New York, Neha Motipara decided to create her own to send to family and friends. "I used a traditional wooden block already carved with a motif that I purchased on a recent trip to India," she explains. "Block printing is an old Indian art form and adds a traditional element to an otherwise Western approach to expressing celebratory feelings. For the stock I chose a natural-colored, fibrous cover with bronze flecks

to add to the earthiness of the traditional printing process. The overall production for the 30-card print run included printing a greeting on the exterior and interior of the card with a home printer, mixing custom inks, block printing the motifs and, as a finishing touch, adding fine bronze glitter to specific sections of the motif. I then customized each card with a personalized message."

Thanksgiving Promotion

★ ★

Studio
Turnstyle

Design
Steve Watson, Bryan Mamaril,
Jason Gómez

Client
CK Graphics

Format
Calendar

Country
USA

Thanksgiving (celebrated on the fourth Thursday in November in the USA and the second Monday in October in Canada) is now primarily a social event at which family and friends join for a festive meal, nearly always featuring turkey. Unlike many other celebrations, the visual or graphic element is muted, with attention instead focused on the culinary aspects—reflecting its origins as a harvest feast. However,

Thanksgiving can have a graphic expression, as in this promotional October to December calendar created for Seattle printing company CK Graphics. Designed by local design group Turnstyle, it presents each month as a "flatpack" character that people can build and display on their desktops. The November character is a turkey and the October creature a Halloween monster, while December is represented by a reindeer.

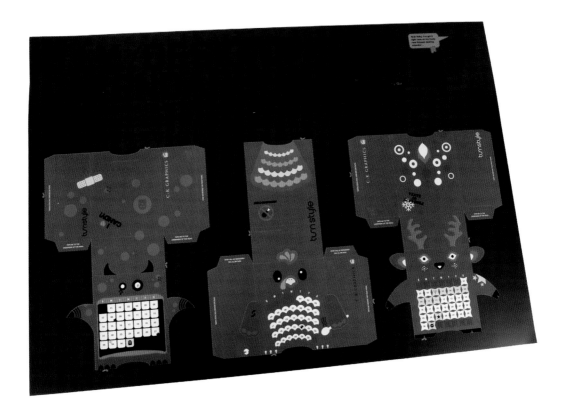

FESTIVAL FACTS

BONFIRE NIGHT

- "Remember, remember the fifth of November …" Thus goes the ditty reminding Brits of the so-called Gunpowder Plot of 1605, an attempt by Roman Catholics to blow up the Houses of Parliament in London and overthrow Protestantism.

- The conspirators, including Guy Fawkes, were stopped in their tracks when 36 kegs of gunpowder were discovered under the House of Lords. The event, known either as Bonfire Night or Guy Fawkes' Night, has since become one of the most popular festivals in the UK, and is generally seen as an excuse for private and public fireworks and bonfires.

- In a practice that is dying out, children create effigies known as "guys" and collect money for their efforts before the effigies are torched. The event is celebrated with particular fervor in the southern English town of Lewes, where effigies of Catholic or topical figures are burnt alongside those of Guy Fawkes.

© Dominic Alves

Bonfire Night in Lewes, UK

STAR OF BETHNAL GREEN -- NOVEMBER GUIDE
359 BETHNAL GREEN ROAD
LONDON E2 6LG

THIS MOTHS STAR OF BETHNAL GREEN IS
SOLIS LAUNDERETTE 335 BETHNAL GREEN
ROAD AND THEY DO, DO DUVETS!

TO NOMINATE YOUR OWN STAR OF BETHNAL
GREEN JUST DROP US A MAIL

FOR BOOKINGS & GENERAL ENQUIRIES
TELEPHONE +44 (0)207 729 0167
INFO@STAROFBETHNALGREEN.COM
WWW.STAROFBETHNALGREEN.COM

Bonfire Night Poster

★ ★ ★ ★ ★ ★ ★ ★ ★ ★ ★ ★ ★ ★ ★

Design
Bunch Design

Client
The Star of Bethnal Green

Format
Flyer, poster

Country
UK

The Star of Bethnal Green is a
popular bar and club in the East End
of London. As part of promotional
activities for the venue, Bunch Design
created a monthly series of posters
and flyers that play with its name
both visually and verbally. Each
month a local "star" is nominated
and mentioned (in this case a local
launderette), and the visuals showcase
a specific theme using stars. This
proved particularly suitable for the
November design, which showcased
Bonfire Night (November 5) with
a firework display in the shape of a
star over the night lights of London.
The flyers and posters have become
collectibles for the regulars of the bar.

© Tomas Castelazo

© Charles & Josette Lenars/CORBIS

FESTIVAL FACTS

DIA DE LOS MUERTOS

- Dia de los Muertos is the Mexican Day of the Dead. Commemorating the dead is an important feature of most cultures, but is something that Mexicans, both inside and outside the country, treat with astonishing visual impact.

- As in other cultures people visit cemeteries, clean graves, and leave offerings for the departed, but in Mexico on the Dia de los Muertos everywhere erupts with joyously decorated skulls and skeletons. These lavishly decorated items are intended to coax the dead back and to reassure the souls that they have come to the right place. Rather than being eerie, the images encourage a reassuring engagement with the departed, and often a humorous, mocking tone is adopted rather than one of solemnity and fear.

- While Christian in format, the Dia de los Muertos is a festival that also has clear links with various ancient Mexican cultures and rites.

- The Dia de los Muertos is a bit of a misnomer as it is held over two days—All Saint's Day and All Soul's Day—which fall on November 1 and 2 in the Western Christian calendar, and in the days and weeks that lead up to these days. The first day is dedicated to children who have died, and the following day to departed adults. Many people spend the year preparing for this event.

- The *calavera* or skull is the principal symbol of the Dia de los Muertos. Ghoulish imagery abounds, and skulls are decorated in bright colors according to folkloric traditions. Apart from two-dimensional depictions, various skeleton dolls are made, and masks or mannequins produced with papier-mâché. Confectionary skulls, either made of sugar or chocolate, are also eaten, mainly by children. Marionettes with *calavera* heads or skeletal bodies are another popular manifestation. The *calavera* cartoons of nineteenth-century illustrator José Guadalupe Posada continue to inspire much of the artwork.

Left: Models of Catrinas, inspired by José Guadalupe Posada, at Museo de la Ciudad, Leon, Guanajuato, Mexico

Above: An army of happy skeletons made from papier-mâché

Dia de los Muertos Promotion ‹

★ ★ ★ ★ ★ ★ ★ ★ ★ ★ ★ ★ ★ ★ ★

Design
Collette Wallace

Client
Yvonne Reineman

Format
Poster

Country
USA

Skulls and skeletons have long functioned as "memento mori," or reminders of our mortality. In Mexican culture, the skull or *calavera* is the main image for the important Dia de los Muertos. These two traditions were brought together by celebrated Mexican illustrator José Guadalupe Posada (who died in 1913) in one of his most famous images, that of Catrina. A wealthy, fashionably dressed woman festooned with a large hat, her face is rendered as a skull to show the transience of life and the futility of vanity. It's an image that became so iconic that it has continued to inspire a whole category of "Catrinas," either drawn or crafted as models. This poster, entitled "La Catrina," follows in the tradition. The *calavera* was hand-drawn, then tweaked in Photoshop and Illustrator.

FESTIVAL FACTS

EID UL-ADHA

- "Eid" is Arabic for "festival," and the word refers to two important events for Muslims. Eid el-Fitr marks the end of the holy month of Ramadan, and Eid ul-Adha, known as the Greater Eid, is an extended festivity to mark the end of the pilgrimage to Mecca, or the Hajj.

- Eid ul-Adha is the second most important day for Muslims, and is celebrated whether or not people have been able to make the pilgrimage.

- Public prayer meetings take place and feasts are prepared from freshly slaughtered animals. The feast celebrates the occasion when the Prophet Ibrahim was willing to sacrifice his own son—Allah intervened and a lamb was slaughtered instead.

- Charity for the poor and disadvantaged, whether in the form of food or money, is a central aspect of Eid.

- Eid ul-Adha takes place on the tenth day of the Islamic month of Dhul-Hijjah, which varies according to the Gregorian calendar.

Eid ul-Adha Cards

★ ★

Design
Vaishali Shah at Creative ID

Photography
David West

Client
Various

Format
Cards

Country
UK

As there are two Muslim festivals known as Eid, and the visual approach is traditionally abstract, designs can function equally well for Eid el-Fitr (see pp 160–161) and Eid ul-Adha, which marks the end of the Hajj, or pilgrimage to Mecca. These cards are designed for British Muslims and carry an explanation of the festivals.

While remaining true to traditional requirements, they also introduce colors beyond the traditional green, as well as motifs such as lotus flowers, mosaics, and minaret patterns, alongside script-based decoration.

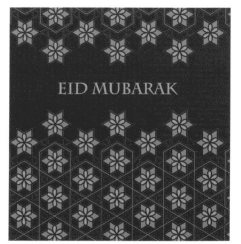

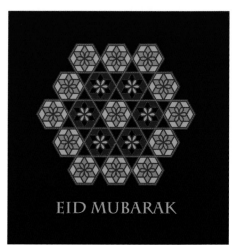

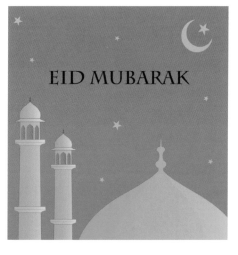

December

1st: World AIDS Day (pp 194–197)

Hanukkah (pp 198–199)

6th: St. Nikolaos Day - Greece

6th: Independence Day - Finland

13th: Lucia Day - festival of light, Sweden

20th–23rd: Winter Solstice - northern hemisphere

25th: Christmas Day (pp 200–243)

26th–Jan 1st: Kwanzaa (pp 244–245)

FESTIVAL FACTS

WORLD AIDS DAY

- In response to the devastating AIDS pandemic, two officials at the World Health Organization came up with the idea of World AIDS Day as a global event that could be staged annually to focus attention on the suffering the disease was causing and to mobilize efforts to combat it.

- World AIDS Day was first held on December 1, 1988 and has been marked on the same day each year since. Concerts, campaigns, political speeches, fundraising events, and memorials to those who have died of HIV/AIDS all combine to make up the somber event.

- In 2007, nearly 33 million people were living with the disease and that year alone 2 million people died from it. The day is now officially organized by the World AIDS Campaign.

- The Red Ribbon, worn as an act of solidarity with those who have HIV and those who have died as a result of HIV and AIDS, has become one of the most identifiable and copied of symbols. It was devised by Visual Aids, a New York artistic collective, in 1991. Either actual folded red ribbon or a representation is used. Different colors of the same symbol have since been used for other awareness-raising campaigns, such as pink ribbons for breast cancer.

The shape of the Red Ribbon being made with 1,000 pairs of handprints to mark World AIDS Day in Hefei, capital of east China's Anhui Province

Volunteers signed up for activities they would
like to be involved in with VSO-organized
Dance4Life World AIDS Day celebration

World AIDS Day T-shirt

★ ★ ★ ★ ★ ★ ★ ★ ★ ★ ★ ★ ★ ★ ★

Design

Sergio Magalhães, Miro, Gil França, Paula Reboredo, Adriane Galisteu, Cako Martin

Client

Levi Strauss & Co.

Format

T-shirts

Country

Brazil

Levi has supported World AIDS Day from its inception, with various campaigns and initiatives around the world. For Brazil in 2008, it ran a campaign around the idea of "69 with a condom" ("69 com camisinha" in Portuguese). An eclectic cast of designers, including TV celebrity Adriane Galisteu, fashion photographer Miro, fashion impresarios Paula Reboredo and Gil França, designer Sérgio Magalhães, and art director Cako Martin, was asked to design T-shirts in support. The approaches varied from the oversized red ribbon that appears almost as a shawl in the design of Galisteu to the humorous arrow of Magalhães.

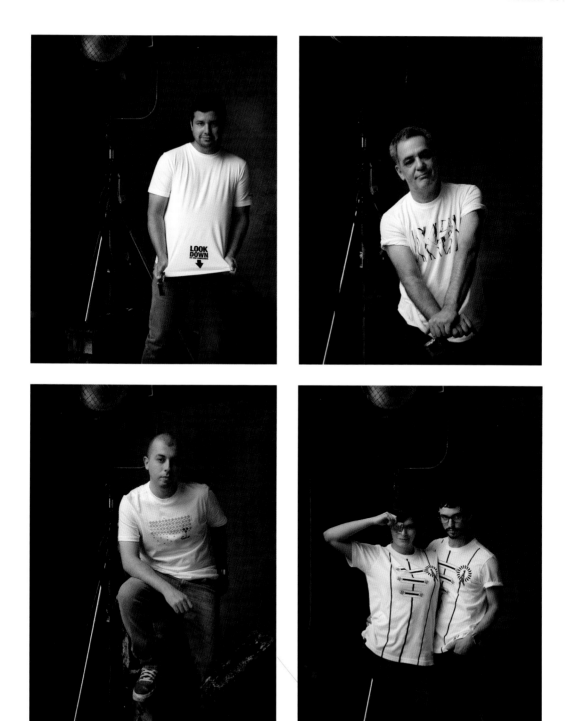

Three fully lit Hanukkah menorahs in
a private home during a celebration

FESTIVAL FACTS

HANUKKAH
(OR CHANUKAH, FESTIVAL OF LIGHTS)

- It may not be the most important of the festivals in the Jewish calendar (Yom Kippur, Rosh Hashanah, and Passover are all more significant), but Hanukkah is the most visual.

- It is a celebration that takes place over eight nights and eight days, and commemorates the re-dedication ("*Hanukkah*" means "dedication" in Hebrew) of the Holy Temple in Jerusalem following a successful revolt against the Syrians in 165 BCE.

- At the time, enough ritual oil to light the candle on the menorah (the traditional Jewish candlestick) for one night only was found, but miraculously, this was able to keep the candle alight for eight nights, thus lending the festival its duration. Each night a new candle is lit on a special nine-branched menorah (the normal menorah has only seven branches), and the sight of these burning candles, placed in windows to be seen by people walking past, acts as a reminder of the original event.

- Hanukkah is celebrated on the 25th of Kislev in the Jewish calendar, which equates to various dates in November and December in the Gregorian calendar.

Eighteenth-century woodcut showing the lighting of
the special nine-branched menorah during Hanukkah.
Produced in Amsterdam in 1723

FESTIVAL FACTS

CHRISTMAS

- Christmas is now the most widely celebrated event around the world. Nominally celebrating the birth of Christ, it is not as important as Easter for devout Christians, but has transcended its origins to become an event that is increasingly observed by atheists and non-Christians around the world.

- Like so many other Western festivals, it has origins in ancient rites (winter festivals) that were co-opted by the church. However, its current form has a distinctly central European and Germanic flavor, as seen, for instance, in the Christmas tree, a fir tree topped with an angel or star and decorated with various ornaments, sometimes made of gingerbread.

- Santa Claus, or Father Christmas, is another figure with roots in Germanic culture, but is of relatively recent origin and commercially very successful. Convention has it that he, often drawn by reindeer, delivers the gifts that children receive. ("Santa Claus" is a corruption of "Saint Nikolaus," a saint who is commemorated on December 6, and whose feast day is still the subject of extensive celebrations in many European countries, often involving children and gifts.)

- The giving of sumptuously packaged gifts, however delivered, makes Christmas the most important date in the calendar for retailers. The giving of Christmas cards to family, friends, and acquaintances is very widely observed.

- The format of the celebration varies considerably according to country and tradition. While Christmas was traditionally a twelve-day festival starting on Christmas Day (December 25), it is now generally limited to Christmas Eve, Christmas Day, and, in some countries, Boxing Day (December 26).

- The many traditions, biblical and folkloric, that feed into Christmas have resulted in a very extensive iconography. However, the Christmas tree in various forms and Santa Claus/Father Christmas are probably the most identifiable images.

- Harking back to its winter festival origins, imagery derived from snow is also popular, not only because of its creative possibilities, but also because it allows for design that does not engage with the event's religious aspects. Mistletoe and holly are images from the natural world that have religious, pagan, and seasonal significance. The Christmas meal, again varying significantly from country to country, also provides images for a graphic representation of Christmas.

- Advent describes the 24-day period leading up to Christmas, and is given graphic presence in the Advent calendar developed by Lutherans in Germany— children could open one window each day to reveal an image or a treat. Advent wreaths feature four candles, one of which is lit on each of the four Sundays leading up to Christmas.

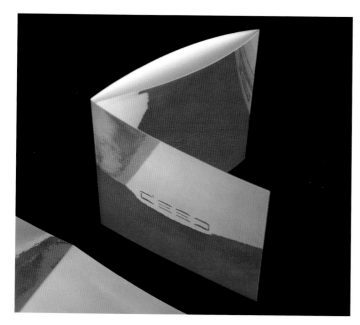

Christmas Mailer

★ ★ ★ ★ ★ ★ ★ ★ ★ ★ ★ ★ ★ ★ ★

Studio
Deep

Design
Grant Bowden

Client
Self-initiated

Format
Card

Country
UK

For this card, design consultancy Deep chose a design based on wordplay around its name. The words "deep" and "freeze" were embossed on the card, which was chosen from special iridescent, mirror-effect stock to reflect colors "like petrol in water or frozen ice," says Grant Bowden at Deep. The special effect is picked up by the message inside, which says "Wishing you a colorful Christmas."

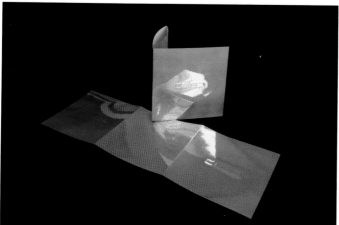

Christmas Decorations

★ ★ ★ ★ ★ ★ ★ ★ ★ ★ ★ ★ ★ ★ ★

Design
Nikolaus Schmidt

Client
Self-initiated

Format
Card, poster, gift wrap

Country
Austria

If Christmas is a time of giving, it is also a test of a graphic designer's skills, as anything emanating from their studio will require originality and be scrutinized even more closely than usual. Austrian graphic designer Nikolaus Schmidt created a design that was used for Christmas cards, a poster, and gift wrap. He managed to achieve striking modern effects, yet used very traditional means to achieve this. A simple triangle representing a pared-down Christmas tree is repeated at different sizes to create the shimmering presence of a larger tree.

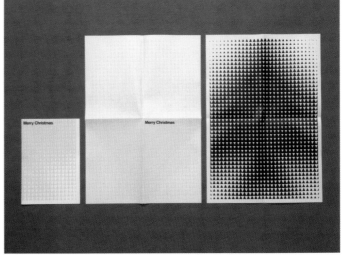

Holiday Party Invitation

★ ★

Studio
TFI Envision Inc.

Design
Elizabeth P. Ball

Client
Self-initiated

Format
Gift box

Country
USA

In North America, the holiday season is interpreted loosely in order to join the various winter festivities. There is no fixed definition, but it always includes Christmas and New Year, and often Thanksgiving as well. TFI Envision, a design group in Connecticut, holds a holiday party every year and uses the invitations not only to entice people, but also to show what it can do. Sent out in the form of gift boxes with labels, the recipient opened them one year to find a tiny, hand-assembled invitation with pictograms incorporating tiny type. A magnifying glass on a satin cord allowed the invitation to be deciphered. Another year the box opened to reveal a diorama of a snowy winter night scene.

Christmas Greetings and Decoration

★ ★

Design

Selin Ozguzer

Client

Self-initiated

Format

Card

Country

USA

If unwrapping and surprise are central to the experience of Christmas, then this card participates to the full. Whetting the appetite with a silver bubble-foil envelope, the card initially presents itself as a folded red square that opens up like a poinsettia, a traditional Christmas pot plant. Within this another white square, rotated by 45°, opens up to reveal a small Christmas tree at the center

of the flowerlike design. The tree is picked out in silver and decorated with baubles (in reality metal eyelets), with colorful, self-adhesive dots behind them. A further eyelet on the outer card allows it to be hung and become a Christmas-tree decoration itself.

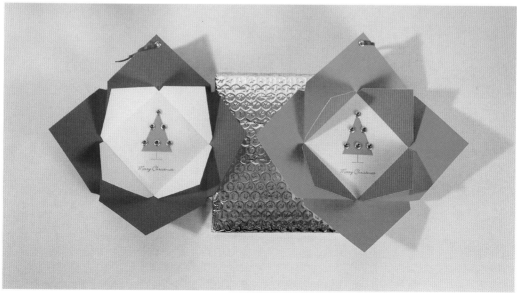

Christmas Display

★ ★ ★ ★ ★ ★ ★ ★ ★ ★ ★ ★ ★ ★ ★

Design
Deep

Client
Lend Lease

Format
Lightbox

Country
UK

Lend Lease is a global property company, and its London head office wanted something special to celebrate Christmas. Deep came up with a lightbox situated in its entrance lobby to welcome people to the building with greetings in many different languages, and with the shape of a Christmas tree etched out as if by a festive sparkler.

Christmas Book

★ ★ ★ ★ ★ ★ ★ ★ ★ ★ ★ ★ ★ ★ ★

Studio
ZORA Identity &
Interaction Design

Design and Art Direction
Steffi Pohl, Britta Boland

Client
Self-initiated (in collaboration
with Tipografia Gianotti)

Format
Hardback book

Country
Germany

While Christmas is celebrated across
Europe, each country has its own
individual traditions and, of course,
festive recipes. ZORA, a design group
in Düsseldorf, Germany, decided to
bring these together and celebrate
their differences in a festive book,
which they published trilingually
(in German, Italian, and English).
Twelve different customs and recipes,
from the Netherlands, Sweden,
Hungary, Germany, Finland, Poland,
the Czech Republic, France, England,
Italy, Spain, and Greece, are included.
Each is represented by hand-drawn
illustrations (linked typographically
or thematically with the ingredients),
that have been scanned and digitized.
The book's laminated dust jacket
features a collage from all 12 entries,
and this is repeated on the hard cover,
printed with a UV varnish.

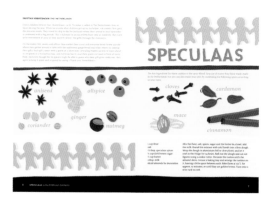

Christmas Greetings

★ ★

Studio
Curious

Design
Gary Smith, Peter Rae, Ben
Wrigley, Louise Desborough,
Joe Harries

Art Direction
Gary Smith, Peter Rae

Copywriting
Des Waddy

Photography
Iain Dickins

Client
Self-initiated

Format
Concertina card

Country
UK

For this Christmas card, design group Curious came up with the idea of a card that would feature various Christmas curiosities "from the traditional to the bizarre." After combing the Internet, the designers settled on eight different weird and wonderful "facts" from around the world, elements of which were then photographed and presented, along with a short tongue-in-cheek description, in a concertina card that could stand on its own. For the front of the card they photographed a cake specially commissioned for the occasion.

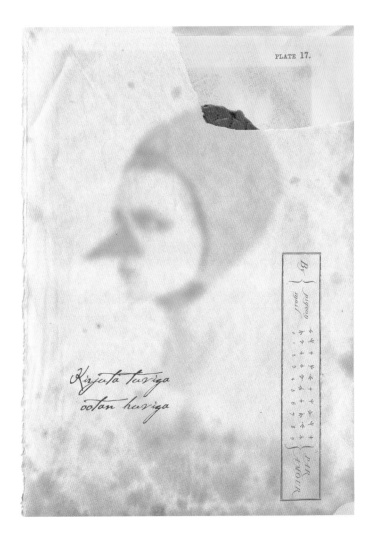

Christmas Greetings

★ ★

Design
Jyri Loun, Ruth Huimerind

Art Direction and Photography
Ruth Huimerind

Client
MAP Estonia

Format
Card

Country
Estonia

Estonian designer and photographer Ruth Huimerind specializes in the kind of slightly surreal montage that makes this a Christmas card with a difference. While Christmassy in its palette, it subverts various traditional images and is humorously captioned "Carrier pigeon" as though culled from an old book.

PLATE 17.

𝔓𝔞𝔳𝔬 𝔯𝔞𝔯𝔲𝔰

[haruldane jõululind, huviline kirjatuviline]

Seasons Greetings

Christmas Greetings

★ ★ ★ ★ ★ ★ ★ ★ ★ ★ ★ ★ ★ ★ ★ ★ ★

Design

Netra Nei

Client

Urban Ease

Format

Card

Country

USA

For Urban Ease, a retailer of
modern furniture and kitchens in
Seattle, local design consultancy
Netra Nei produced this unusual
Christmas card. Though it looks
like a photograph, it was hand-
rendered in a 3D modeling program;
the "product" represented (a self-
sufficient Christmas light), is actually
imaginary even though it seems
eminently feasible, and being virtual,
it was easy to print the client's name
on the battery in place of the usual
battery branding.

Christmas Greetings

★ ★

Design
Julie Verhoeven

Photography
Emily Keegin

Client
Royal College of Art, London

Format
Card

Country
UK

Every year the Royal College of Art (RCA), the postgraduate art and design school in London, invites one of its former students to design a limited-edition Christmas card, the proceeds of which go to its student fund. For this card the task was entrusted to Julie Verhoeven, an illustrator who has specialized in working with fashion brands such as Versace, Mulberry, and John Galliano, and who also teaches fashion at the RCA. Entitled "Ho, Ho, Ho," the card consists of Christmas paraphernalia such as baubles, glitter, and candles, interspersed with coins and bottle tops, all of which surround an illustration of a woman's face. The result is an unusual and arresting image that remains immediately identifiable with the festivities of Christmas.

 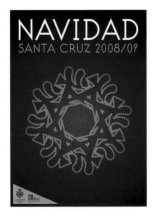 

Christmas City Decorations

★ ★

Studio
Design by Lars

Design
Lars Amundsen

Client
Santa Cruz de Tenerife local
government

Format
Posters, postcard,
press advertising

Country
Spain

Christmas street decoration is a
well-established tradition in most
Christian countries, with retailers
and local governments often working
together to create festive lighting
or other outdoor decorations for the
Advent period. In Spain, Christmas is
celebrated with particular gusto, from
the beginning of Advent (the fourth
Sunday before Christmas Day) right
up to the Feast of the Magi (*Los
Reyes Magos* in Spanish, celebrating
the arrival of the Three Wise Men)

on January 6. The local government
of Santa Cruz, the capital of Tenerife
in the Canary Islands, wanted
a festive campaign to contribute to
the celebration which, because of the
island's balmy climate, includes many
outdoor events. Lars Amundsen was
commissioned to come up with these
luminescent designs, taking up space
that would otherwise be used for
banal advertising. "To simulate
conventional Christmas lighting
in shopping areas, I manipulated

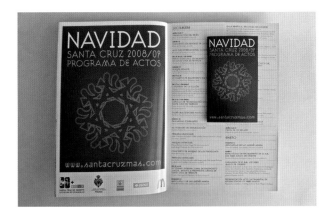

★ ★ ★ ★ ★ ★ ★ ★ ★ ★ ★ ★ ★ ★ ★

a set of decorative illustrations
in Adobe Illustrator. By using an
outline with a dashed line stroke
and a gradient fill to add depth and
contrast, I created images with an
almost photographic quality,"
explains Amundsen. The approach
was supported by a five-color print
process on high-gloss paper, to create
a modern and clean, yet very festive
street decoration.

Christmas and New Year Greetings

★ ★

Studio
Form

Design
Arran Lidgett, Paul West,
Paula Benson

Client
Self-initiated

Format
Web home page, poster, mailer

Country
UK

Form, a graphic design consultancy, has extensive bookshelves running down one side of its studio. These proved the unlikely inspiration for this Christmas and New Year card. Shelves were partially emptied to leave only a handful of books and examples of Form's work to make the shape of a Christmas tree. "For New Year, we put the studio back into order, retaining a few elements of the Christmas tree," says Paul West, cofounder of Form. "The double-sided poster uses a thin stock to allow show-through, so the Christmas and New Year images were visible against each other in the light. We also created a video of the event and uploaded it to our website as 'behind the scenes' footage."

Merry Christmas
from Form®

For more information or if you would like to see the
Form® portfolio please phone Paul West or Paula Benson
on +44 (0)20 7014 1430 or email studio@form.uk.com.

To see examples of our work in music, media, branding
and many areas of contemporary culture please see
www.form.uk.com.

Christmas Greetings

★ ★

Studio
Studio International

Design
Boris Ljubicic

Client
SMS

Format
Card

Country
Croatia

Among other things, food company SMS makes various dried-fruit spreads, the packaging of which has fingerprints on it, picking up on the telltale signs of someone succumbing to the temptation of dipping their finger into an open jar. So when it came to designing a Christmas card for the company, Boris Ljubicic chose to take this idea further and created a card that features a Christmas tree composed of sticky fingerprints.

Christmas Display

★ ★

Studio
Fluid

Design
Lee Basford

Animation
SGUD

Client
Adam et Ropé

Format
Animation

Country
UK/Japan

For Adam et Ropé, a Japanese fashion company, Lee Basford created a Christmas decoration with a difference. Deliberately childlike handmade shapes and objects were made into a charming, short linear narrative for an in-store, on-screen animation. Part of the design formed the basis for a downloadable card for *PingMag*, a Japanese online design magazine. The animation also served as a tutorial in the UK magazine *Computer Arts*.

Christmas
Campaign ⊹
★ ★ ★ ★ ★ ★ ★ ★ ★ ★ ★ ★ ★ ★ ★ ★

Studio
AmoebaCorp

Design and Art Direction
Lora Leclair, Mike Kelar

Illustration
Sanjai Bhama, Lora Leclair

Photography
Christopher Wadsworth

Client
The Bay

Format
Bags, banners

Country
Canada

The Bay is one of Canada's largest retailers. It asked AmoebaCorp to develop an engaging, extensive, and festive Christmas campaign that could be used both in-store and across all its communications. "The stag featured on the front of the bag became the 'icon' of the campaign," explains AmoebaCorp's Mike Kelar. "The interpretation of the stag was a strategic move to convey the relationship of the Canadian landscape with the magic of Christmas in a nontraditional way. The overall color scheme of darker shades of red and blue was chosen to give the traditional Christmas red a more sophisticated feel and illustrate the feeling of the 'magic forest' in moonlight." Uncoated paper stocks were used for the shopping and gift bags "to emphasize the tactility of the Canadian outdoors. It was also important to design a bag that would be kept as a gift-giving bag, past its standard use as a shopping bag," Kelar adds.

Nativity Scene

★ ★

Design
Marcello Jori,
Massimo Giacon

Client
Alessi

Format
Porcelain figurines

Country
Italy

Few countries put as much love and dedication into Christmas nativity scenes as Italy, with the southern city of Naples particularly famous for its market selling figurines for nativity displays. While traditionally the figures are carved from wood,

Italian design company Alessi, most famous for its homeware designs, commissioned designers Marcello Jori and Massimo Giacon to develop modern alternatives in a style in keeping with the rest of its products, and made from porcelain.

Christmas Stationery ✦

★ ★ ★ ★ ★ ★ ★ ★ ★ ★ ★ ★ ★ ★ ★

Studio
Unreal

Design
Brian Eagle, Kevin Grennan,
Mat Giles, Lee Burns, Jodie
Wightman

Art Direction
Brian Eagle

Client
Self-initiated

Format
Gift wrap

Country
UK

Like an increasing number of graphic
design groups, Unreal has an online
shop as a lighthearted sideline. For
Christmas 2008, it stocked six
different wrapping papers designed
by its team, which were intended not
only to be witty and attractive, but
also interactive. The designs reference
British Christmas traditions, such
as "spot the Christmas sixpence
pudding" (traditionally the Christmas
pudding was stirred by the whole
family and everyone made a wish,
which would come true for the
person whose portion contained
the sixpence coin). Another features
a "Queen's speech bingo" (the
broadcast of the Queen's speech
on Christmas Day is a fixture in many
British homes), while others show
a flow-chart of popular gifts and a list
of pawnbrokers for unwanted presents.

Christmas Party Invitation

★ ★

Studio
Vanity's Edge

Design
Alana Beall

Client
Baltimore Steel Erectors

Format
Invitation

Country
USA

As with many companies, Baltimore Steel Erectors in Maryland held a Christmas party for its clients, suppliers, and employees. Local designer Alana Beall was tasked with coming up with a Christmas card that would also function as an enticing invitation. Sticking to the traditional Christmas colors of red and green, the design opens out to show Santa and his elves as workers on a construction site, as a humorous nod in the direction of the business of the company.

Christmas Display

★ ★

Studio
Studio Output

Design
Stewart McMillan

Photography
Nisbet Wylie

Client
USC

Format
Window display

Country
UK

USC is a youth fashion retailer with 30 stores around the UK. It was looking for something Christmassy for its shop windows for the festive period, but wanted something that would resonate with its target audience. Rather than go for traditional festive imagery, Studio Output decided to look at the Christmas party and its reputation for getting people to let their hair down a little more than they intended. The designers describe it as "a tongue-in-cheek look at the Christmas party, and how it develops over the course of an evening." The images were used at very large sizes in USC's store windows for maximum impact.

Christmas Rebrand

★ ★ ★ ★ ★ ★ ★ ★ ★ ★ ★ ★ ★ ★ ★

Studio
Pentagram Design, New York

Design
Don Bilodeau, Julia Hoffmann,
Armin Vit, Michael Yi

Art Direction
James Biber, Michael Bierut,
Michael Gericke, Luke
Hayman, Abbott Miller,
Paula Scher, Lisa Strausfeld

Client
Studio 360

Format
Brand manual

Country
USA

Christmas can be a victim of its own
success. To excite the jaded palate
and bored consumer Studio 360,
a cultural radio program, decided
to get the designers at Pentagram's
New York offices to approach
a rebrand of Christmas as though
it were an ordinary commercial brief.
"With tongues planted firmly in their
cheeks," the team came up with
a comprehensive and humorous
redesign, comprising many different
aspects, from a variable naming
strategy and the domain name
".mas" (thought up by Paula Scher
and Lisa Strausfeld), through to
a new, universal icon (by James
Biber), variations on the Christmas
tree (Abbott Miller's contribution),
and downloadable wrapping paper
(designed by Luke Hayman).

Tree alternatives

The icon: A cone

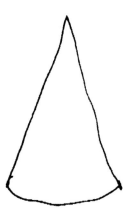

Bells

White "cone" cake

Ice "cone" tray

Candles

"... and cones were hung
by the chimney with care."

At home flatpack version

Cone snowman hat

Lighted cone trees

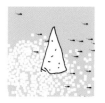

Sugar loaf cone

"Ikea" cone

Christmas Greetings

★ ★ ★ ★ ★ ★ ★ ★ ★ ★ ★ ★ ★ ★ ★

Design
Jyri Loun, Ruth Huimerind

Art Direction and Photography
Ruth Huimerind

Client
MAP Estonia

Format
Envelopes

Country
Estonia

The post offices of many countries issue special Christmas stamps, so Estonian designer Ruth Huimerind decided to do something similar. These Christmas envelopes are adorned with pretend stamps, with various lighthearted and multilingual one-liners. The envelopes are further adorned with semi-official blind embossing, which says "The snow is talking to you."

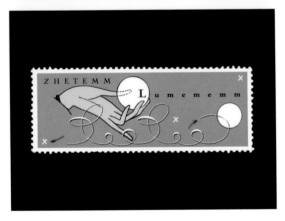

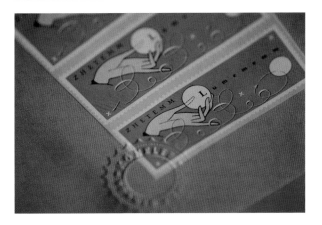

Christmas Party Invitation

★ ★

Studio
Transfer Studio

Design
Falko Grentrup,
Valeria Hedman

Client
Self-initiated

Format
Cup holder

Country
UK

For a Christmas party at their studio in London, Swedish expats Falko Grentrup and Valeria Hedman hit upon the idea of an invitation that would be festive as well as functional. While setting the mood and giving the requisite information, the invite would also double as a festive and heat-insulating holder for the paper cup containing Christmas mulled wine or glögg. "After a time of great creative work, your brain, spirit, and body need a break," they say, "especially if you are in the middle of winter and the dark and cold is getting to you. Joined by friends and colleagues, we adopted the Swedish tradition of celebrating by feasting on homemade saffron buns washed down with mulled wine. The simple paper cup holder, usually a mundane object, instantly conveys what to expect—a warm and cosy break on a cold December day."

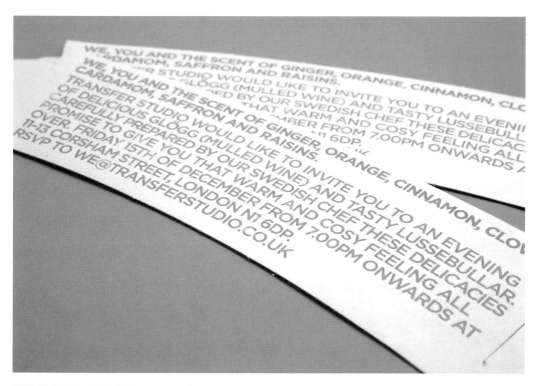

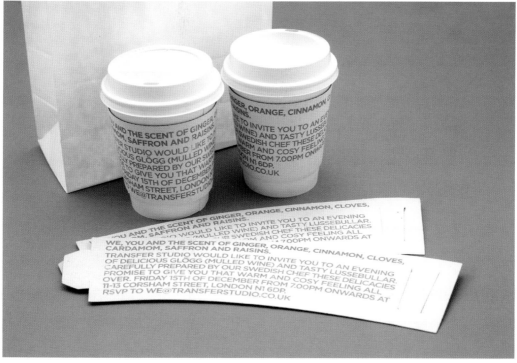

Christmas Greetings and Decoration

★ ★

Design

Nick Clark Design

Client

Self-initiated

Format

Card

Country

UK

Most Christmas cards have just a brief life before being consigned to the trash can or recycling bin, so in this card Nick Clark decided to suggest recycling in a lighthearted way. "The Christmas card doubles as a festive tree or a paper plane,"

he explains. "Basically, it was really only a printed sheet of paper with folding guidelines and instructions on how to throw it away."

Christmas Greetings

★ ★

Studio
Turnstyle

Design
Madeleine Eiche

Client
Teague

Format
Card

Country
USA

For its 2007 Christmas card, Teague, a design company specializing in industrial product design, turned to graphic designers Turnstyle, who are also based in Seattle. They came up with a card that plays ingeniously with traditional snow imagery by screenprinting in white on "warm" off-white felt. This very tactile card was then posted out in a transparent envelope, which added another layer of sensory intrigue.

FESTIVAL FACTS

KWANZAA

- Kwanzaa is a recent, specifically Afro-American holiday established in 1966 by activist Maulana Karenga, aiming to create a framework in which black Americans can reconnect with lost African heritage and celebrate their communal culture and values. It has since developed to be celebrated more widely in other communities and in different countries.

- Kwanzaa is celebrated over seven days (from December 26 to January 1) and takes its cue from harvest celebrations. Its name is derived from Swahili, the widely spoken African language, and the phrase "*matunda ya kwanza*" or first fruits. Each of the seven days represents one of the seven different principles that make up Kwanzaa: unity, self-determination, collective work and responsibility, cooperative economics, purpose, creativity, and faith.

- According to The Organization Us, the official custodian of the festivity, the principal colors of the festival are green, red, and black (considered to be pan-African colors and used in many African flags). Symbols include the seven candles (*Mishumaa Saba*), crops and corn (*Mazao* and *Muhindi*), the mat (*Mkeka*) and the cup of unity (*Kikombe cha Umoja*).

Kwanzaa Stamps ›

★ ★ ★ ★ ★ ★ ★ ★ ★ ★ ★ ★ ★ ★ ★

Design
Daniel Minter

Client
US Postal Service

Format
Postage stamp

Country
USA

Kwanzaa, the week-long celebration of African heritage by Afro-Americans, was first commemorated by the US Postal Service in 1997, and again in 2004 with a new design by artist and illustrator Daniel Minter. The design consciously draws on traditional African aesthetics, and the seven principles that underlie the seven-day festivity. "I used seven figures to represent *Ujima*, which means community," explains Minter. "Two mothers, *Imani*, which means faith, and *Nia*, which means purpose, are holding the community together. One is a physical mother, and one a spiritual mother. Both of them wear crowns of fabric to distinguish themselves, and atop each crown is a bird. This *Sankofa* bird looks to the past to understand the present, and never forgets whence it came. They are *Kuumba*, or creativity, ready to fly." The stamp has been reissued a number of times by the US Postal Service in subsequent years.

World National Days (fixed date)

	January		February		March
1	Cuba, Haiti, Sudan	1		1	Bosnia and Herzegovina, Wales
2		2		2	Morocco
3		3		3	Bulgaria
4		4	Sri Lanka	4	
5		5		5	
6		6	New Zealand, Niue, Sami	6	Ghana
7		7	Grenada	7	
8	Northern Mariana Islands	8		8	
9		9		9	
10		10		10	
11		11	Japan	11	
12		12		12	Mauritius
13		13		13	
14		14		14	
15		15	Serbia	15	Hungary
16		16	Lithuania	16	
17		17		17	Ireland, Northern Ireland
18		18	Gambia, Nepal	18	Aruba
19		19		19	
20		20		20	Tunisia
21		21		21	Namibia
22		22		22	
23		23	Brunei, Guyana	23	
24		24	Estonia	24	
25		25	Kuwait	25	Greece
26	Australia, India	26		26	Bangladesh
27		27	Dominican Republic	27	
28	Pakistan	28		28	
29				29	
30				30	
31	Nauru			31	Malta, Virgin Islands

April		May		June	
1	Iran, Uzupis	1	Marshall Islands	1	Samoa
2		2		2	Italy
3	Guinea	3	Poland	3	
4	Senegal	4		4	Tonga
5		5	Netherlands	5	Denmark
6		6		6	Sweden
7		7		7	Malta
8		8		8	Norfolk Island
9		9	Channel Islands	9	
10		10		10	Portugal
11		11		11	
12		12		12	The Philippines, Russia
13		13		13	
14		14	Paraguay	14	Falkland Islands
15		15		15	
16		16		16	
17	American Samoa, Syria	17	Norway	17	Iceland
18	Zimbabwe	18		18	Seychelles
19		19		19	
20		20	Cameroon, East Timor	20	
21		21		21	Greenland
22		22	Yemen	22	
23	England	23		23	Luxembourg
24	Vatican City	24	Bermuda, Eritrea	24	
25	Australia, New Zealand	25	Argentina, Jordan	25	Croatia, Mozambique, Slovenia
26	Tanzania	26	Georgia	26	Madagascar
27	Sierra Leone, South Africa, Togo	27		27	Djibouti
28		28	Armenia, Azerbaijan, Ethiopia	28	
29		29	Nigeria	29	
30	Netherlands, Netherlands Antilles	30	Anguilla	30	
		31			

World National Days (fixed date)

	July		August		September
1	British Virgin Islands, Burundi, Canada, Hong Kong, Rwanda	1	Benin, Switzerland	1	Libya, Slovakia, Uzbekistan
2	Curaçao	2		2	Transnistria, Vietnam
3	Belarus	3		3	San Marino
4	USA	4	Burkina Faso, Cook Islands	4	
5	Isle of Man, Venezuela	5		5	
6	Comoros, Malawi	6	Bolivia	6	Bonaire, Swaziland
7	Solomon Islands	7	Côte d'Ivoire	7	Brazil
8		8		8	Andorra, Macedonia, North Korea
9	Argentina, Palau	9	Singapore	9	Tajikistan
10	Bahamas	10	Ecuador	10	Belize, Gibraltar
11	Mongolia	11	Chad	11	
12	Kiribati, São Tomé and Príncipe	12		12	Cape Verde
13	Montenegro	13		13	
14	France, French departments/territories	14		14	
15		15	India, Liechtenstein, Congo, South Korea	15	Costa Rica, El Salvador, Guatemala, Honduras, Nicaragua
16		16	Dominican Republic	16	Mexico, Papua New Guinea
17		17	Gabon, Indonesia	17	
18		18		18	Chile
19		19	Afghanistan	19	St. Kitts and Nevis
20	Colombia	20	Hungary	20	
21	Belgium, Guam	21		21	Belize, Malta
22		22		22	Mali
23	Egypt	23		23	Saudi Arabia
24		24	Ukraine	24	Guinea-Bissau
25	Puerto Rico	25	Uruguay	25	
26	Liberia	26		26	
27		27	Moldova	27	
28	Peru	28		28	
29	Faroe Islands	29	Slovakia	29	
30	Vanuatu	30	Tartarstan, Turks and Caicos Islands	30	Botswana
31		31	Kyrgyzstan, Malaysia, Trinidad and Tobago		

October		November		December	
1	China, Cyprus, Nigeria, Tuvalu	1	Algeria, Antigua and Barbuda	1	Central African Republic, Romania
2	India	2		2	Laos, United Arab Emirates
3	Germany, Iraq	3	Dominica, Micronesia, Panama	3	Saba
4	Lesotho	4		4	
5		5		5	Thailand
6	Egypt	6		6	Finland
7		7		7	
8		8		8	
9	Uganda	9	Cambodia	9	
10	Fiji, Taiwan	10		10	
11		11	Angola, Poland, St. Maarten	11	
12	Equatorial Guinea, Spain	12		12	
13		13		13	Malta, St. Lucia
14		14	Myanmar	14	
15		15		15	Netherlands
16		16	St. Eustatius	16	Bahrain, Kenya
17		17		17	Bhutan
18		18	Latvia, Oman	18	Niger, Qatar
19		19	Monaco	19	
20		20		20	Macau
21	Somalia	21		21	
22		22	Lebanon	22	
23	Hungary	23		23	
24	Zambia	24		24	
25	Kazakhstan	25	Bosnia and Herzegovina, Suriname	25	
26	Austria	26		26	
27	St. Vincent and the Grenadines, Turkmenistan	27		27	
28	Czech Republic, Greece	28	Albania, Mauritania	28	Nepal
29	Turkey	29		29	
30		30	Barbados, Scotland	30	
31				31	

Contributors

★ ★

Alana Beall @ Vanity's Edge
www.vanitysedgedesign.com

AmoebaCorp
www.amoebacorp.com

Marian Bantjes
www.bantjes.com

Because
www.koeweidenpostma.com

Blue River Design
www.blueriver.co.uk

Jason Bolton
www.jasonbolton.com

Brighten the Corners
www.brightenthecorners.com

Browns
www.brownsdesign.com

Bunch Design
www.bunchdesign.com

CHK Design
www.chkdesign.com

Nick Clark Design
www.nickclarkdesign.co.uk

Cowley Design
www.cowleydesign.com

Creative ID
www.creative-id.com

Ellen Crimi-Trent
http://ellencrimitrent.typepad.com

Curious
www.curiouslondon.com

Deep
www.deep.co.uk

Design Army
www.designarmy.com

Design by Lars
www.designbylars.com

Deuce Design
www.deucedesign.com.au

Moham Eissa
www.flickr.com/photos/mohamedeissa/

Electrolychee
www.electrolychee.com

Elfen
www.elfen.co.uk

EMMI
www.emmi.co.uk

Erretres
www.erretres.com

Nicholas Felton
www.feltron.com

Form
www.form-uk.com

Frost Design
www.frostdesign.com.au

Carol García del Busto
www.carolgb.jazztel.es

Massimo Giacon
www.alessi.com

Carin Goldberg
www.caringoldberg.com

HGV
www.hgv.co.uk

Hellohikimori
www.hellohikimori.com

Ruth Huimerind
www.ruthhuimerind.com

Ian Lynam Design
www.ianlynam.com

Inksurge
www.inksurge.com

InsaneFacilities
www.insanefacilities.com

Institute of Contemporary Arts
www.ica.org.uk

Irving Designs
www.irvingdesigns.com

Marcello Jori
www.alessi.com

Kame Design
www.kamedesign.com

Kanella
www.kanella.com

Kolegram
www.kolegram.com

★ ★

Lobby Design
www.lobbydesign.se

LogoMotives
www.jfisherlogomotives.com

M&E
www.myspace.com/matthewandemelie

Memo Productions, Inc.
www.memo-ny.com

Daniel Minter
www.danielminter.com

Multistorey
www.multistorey.net

Netra Nei
www.netranei.com

Neighbour
www.neighbour-uk.com

Nick Clark Design
www.nickclarkdesign.co.uk

nothingdiluted
www.nothingdiluted.com

Selin Ozguzer
www.selins-inn.com

Paragon Marketing Communications
www.paragonmc.com

Planet Interactive Arts
www.planet-ia.com

playful
www.pabloalfieri.co

Room Corporation
www.roomcorporation.com

Rob Ryan
www.misterrob.co.uk

Satellites Mistaken For Stars
www.satellitesmistakenforstars.com

Nikolaus Schmidt
www.nikolausschmidt.com

Shen Design
www.shendesign.com

Siquis
www.siquis.com

The Small Stakes
www.thesmallstakes.com

Andy Smith
www.asmithillustration.com

Studio International
www.studio-international.com

Studio Output
www.studio-output.com

TFI Envision, Inc.
www.tfienvision.com

Thompson Brand Partners
www.thompsonbrandpartners.com

Topos Graphics
www.toposgraphics.com

Transfer Studio
www.transferstudio.co.uk

Turnstyle
www.turnstylestudio.com

UMS Design Studio
www.umsdesign.com

Unreal
www.unreal-uk.com

Julie Verhoeven
www.rca.ac.uk

Collette Wallace
www.chocollette.com

Waterform Design, Inc.
www.masayonai.com

wemakedesign
www.wemakedesign.com

World Studio, Inc.
www.worldstudioinc.com

ZORA Identity &
Interaction Design
www.zora.com

Index

★ ★

★ ★

About the Author

John Stones is a freelance journalist and former features editor of *Design Week*, where he was also the launch editor of *Interiors*. He has worked for *Icon* and *Marketing Week*, and edited a magazine for Virgin Atlantic.

He has a PhD from the Courtauld Institute of Art in London and is the author of *Total Design Sourcebook: Display*, and *No Rules Logos*, both for RotoVision; and *Very Small Shops* for Laurence King.

Edinburgh Festival

Up-Helly-Aa

Notting Hill Carnival

Glastonbury Festival

Bastille Day

Pilgrimage of Saint Blaise

Nice Carnival

Las Fallas

Vancouver Folk Music Festival

Caribana

Washington Ballet Annual Ball

Burning Man

Mardi Gras

Dia de los Muertos

Virgin Islands Carnival

Asilah Arts Festival

Semana Santa

Garifuna Settlement Day

Durba

Inti Raymi

Festa de Yemanjá

Lord of the Tremors

Carnival

Fiesta de la Virgen de la Candelaria